RACE MIXTURE

in the History of Latin America

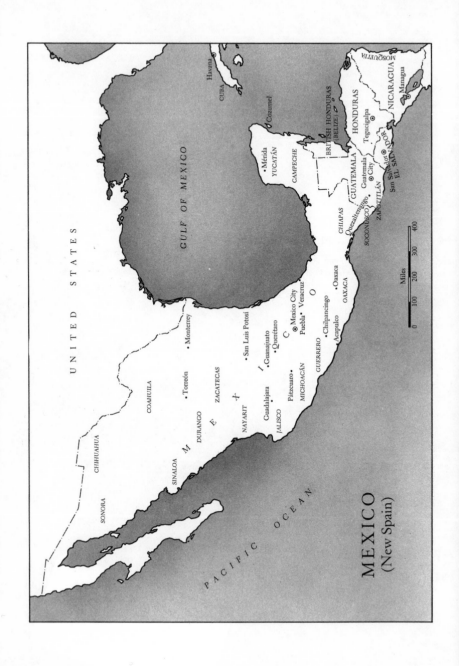

MEXICO
(New Spain)

Havana

CUBA

DOMINICAN REP.

Port-au-Prince · PUERTO RICO

JAMAICA · Kingston

HAITI · Santo Domingo

St. Domingue)

C A R I B B E A N   S E A

BARBADOS

Margarita Is.

Panama City · Coro

Cartagena · Valencia · Caracas

TRINIDAD-TOBAGO

COSTA RICA

San José

PANAMA

Canal

ANTIOQUIA R. · Orinoco R.

Medellín · GUYANA

Cauca Valley · Bogotá · Georgetown

Buenaventura · (Santa Fe) · VENEZUELA · SURINAM · FRENCH GUIANA

Cali

COLOMBIA
(NEW GRANADA)

A T L A N T I C

O C E A N

Equator

ESMERALDAS

ECUADOR · Quito

Guayaquil · Riobamba

· Cuenca

Manaus

Belém · São Luís

PARÁ · Fortaleza

Amazon R.

MARANHÃO

CEARÁ

PERU

B R A Z I L

PERNAMBUCO · Recife

Callao · Lima

Ayacucho

Canudos

Chincha Is. · Cuzco

BOLIVIA

BAHIA · Salvador

Arequipa · (ALTO PERU)

MATO
GROSSO

· La Paz

Brasília

· Santa Cruz de la Sierra

· Sucre (Chuquisaca)

MINAS
GERAIS

· Potosí

PARAGUAY

SÃO PAULO

EL GRAN

São Paulo · Paraíba Valley

CHILE · CHACO · PARANÁ

· Tucumán · Asunción · Rio de Janeiro

MISIONES · RIO GRANDE
DO SUL

Santa Fe · Pôrto Alegre

Córdoba

Valparaíso · Mendoza

Santiago · Rosario

URUGUAY (BANDA ORIENTAL)

Buenos Aires · Montevideo

Concepción · Río de la Plata

P A C I F I C

O C E A N

ARGENTINA

SOUTH AMERICA

Miles

0 100   300   500

A Spanish administrator invites a mestizo, a mulatto, and an Indian for supper. From the Primer Nueva Coronica y Buen Gobierno, *an early seventeenth-century manuscript by the Peruvian Indian Phelipe Guamán Poma de Ayala.*

RACE MIXTURE
in the History of Latin America

MAGNUS MÖRNER
Queens College of the
City University of New York

LITTLE, BROWN AND COMPANY   BOSTON

LIBRARY OF CONGRESS CATALOG CARD NO. 67-24911

TENTH PRINTING

*Published simultaneously in Canada
by Little, Brown & Company (Canada) Limited*

PRINTED IN THE UNITED STATES OF AMERICA

*This book is dedicated to my wife
with gratitude and love*

PREFACE

This is a short book devoted to a very large subject. My purpose is to offer a more or less up-to-date summary based on the present state of research. Such a summary is clearly lacking, and, despite the impressive amount of research carried out in history, anthropology, and sociology, traditional and, in my view, obsolete interpretations continue to dictate much of the popular view on race relations and their historical background in Latin America. As a reaction to this, my views may sometimes be rather sharply expressed, and I hope they will provoke discussion. An intelligent debate is the best way in the pursuit of the truth.

As a result of its summary character, the book is based almost exclusively on secondary works and printed sources, but my familiarity with the unpublished sources on some aspects of the topic has helped to mold my opinions. I am obliged to the students in History 390 at Cornell University in the spring of 1965 for their contributions, their interest, and their intelligent questions, which were stimulating for my work. I also wish to thank the students of history and anthropology who in July, 1965 attended my lectures on the history of race relations at El Colegio de México. Their reaction and our discussions were an enlivening and encouraging experience.

Since Swedish, not English, is my mother tongue, I had my manuscript revised by my old friend, Mr. Albert Read. I am very much obliged to him, as well as to David W. Lynch of Little, Brown for their efforts to improve my English.

MAGNUS MÖRNER

CONTENTS

xi

RACE MIXTURE
in the History of Latin America

The mestizo children of Spanish parish priests being brought to Lima. From Poma de Ayala's chronicle.

I

Race Mixture

In the famous words of José Vasconcelos, the Mexican philosopher, it is in Latin America that a new race will come into being, "made of the treasury of all the previous races, the final race, the cosmic race." It is true that Vasconcelos' words, in his book *Raza Cósmica* (1925), are abstract and cultural.[1] Nevertheless, his vision of a new tropical race does reflect an existing situation. No part of the world has ever witnessed such a gigantic mixing of races as the one that has been taking place in Latin America and the Caribbean since 1492. In fact, it is impossible to determine the racial status of most Latin Americans without a genetic and anthropometric investigation. Toward the end of the eighteenth century, if we are to believe a very knowledgeable historian, miscegenation (used throughout this book in its strictly technical sense), or *mestizaje*, in Spanish, was so advanced in Mexico "that there were few individuals of pure race left in the country." [2] This observation probably could be applied to most parts of Latin America at that time. In that immense region every variation of crosses among the three main stocks, Mongoloids, Caucasoids, and Negroids can be

[1] Vasconcelos (1942), 130. As early as 1916, Vasconcelos called Latin America "fatherland and achievement of mestizos, of two or three races in the blood, by all the cultures in the spirit." Posada (1963).

[2] Borah (1954), 341.

1

found, and everybody there is aware that biological fusion is very real,[3] even though people of dark skin often, it seems, prefer to hint at Indian rather than African ancestry. In some countries mestizaje itself has been transformed, as we shall see later on, into a symbol of nationality.

Many reference works neatly display figures and percentages on the racial composition of Latin American nations. We may find, for example, that 65 per cent of the Venezuelans are mestizos, 20 per cent whites, 8 per cent Negroes, and 7 per cent Indians, or that 9.5 per cent of the Panamanians are Indians, 13.3 per cent Negroes, 11.1 per cent whites, and 65.3 per cent mixed.[4] Such figures are pure guesswork and have no scientific value whatsoever. Even in the few Latin American censuses that use "racial" classifications, the criteria vary greatly, sometimes even between different censuses taken in the same country. The Mexican census of 1929 gave a percentage of 29.2 Indians on the basis of a mostly physical, anthropological criterion. The censuses of 1910 and 1930, based on a socioeconomic criterion, gave 11 per cent and 13 per cent respectively. By applying a linguistic criterion, a Mexican specialist arrived at 15 per cent.[5] It is easy to understand that the abolition of "racial" classification in later censuses is no loss for science.

Though we must give up trying to ascertain exact figures on race, visual observation and some basic knowledge enable us to discern the principal racial patterns of Latin America today. In the Caribbean (except for Puerto Rico) and the northeast of Brazil, the zones in which plantations are found, is an Afro-Latin America. A Euro-Latin America comprises most of Argentina, Uruguay, southernmost Chile, and the south of Brazil; that is, the zone that has received the great waves of European immigrants during the last hundred years. The rest of the region is a Mestizo America with scattered enclaves of indigenous populations in Mexico, Guatemala, and the South American Andes,

[3] This is in striking contrast to the view of the man in the street in Anglo-America. Even people who should know better do not realize how artificial is the "Negro"-"White" dichotomy. See the following journalistic comment on the wife of a "Negro" civil servant: "She is still frequently mistaken for a Caucasian and seldom volunteers a correction. I don't say, Hello, I'm a Negro . . . she says," *Time* (March 4, 1966), 32. The fact is, of course, that Mrs. W. *is* mainly Caucasoid, but that prejudice and tradition, based on what is known about her African descent, classes her as a "Negro." The term "mulatto," rendered useless by its pejorative connotation, has practically disappeared in American usage, leaving a terminological vacuum.

[4] *Information Please Almanac* (New York 1964), 732, 763.

[5] Iturriaga (1951), 93ff.

2

as well as in the Amazon basin. Obviously, there is a close correlation between the racial composition and the climatic and geographic environment. The "Indian" is found today in the Highlands (Sierra) and in low and unproductive tropical zones, the Negro in the low and productive tropical zones, and the white in the low, temperate zones. Even so, the explanation for this racial distribution is mainly historical, as we shall see, starting with the European Conquest and the plantation economy. It might be argued that, from one point of view, the development of race relations and the mestizaje forms the main theme in Latin America's entire history.[6] Even if we admit that the purely "racial" aspect of this history has become less and less conspicuous, it is undeniable that the point of departure, at least, of Latin America's evolution is the meeting on its soil of the Mongoloids, Caucasoids, and Negroids.

Race: A Definition

Approaching this topic, one soon realizes that current terminology obscures the problems instead of clarifying them. The word "race," for instance, can mean almost any human group with certain characteristics in common, especially in literary, rhetorical, propagandistic, or merely everyday language. Only in linguistic and cultural usage, for instance, can we justify the expressions "Germanic race" or "Hispanic race." Properly speaking, "race" should be reserved to designate one of the great divisions of mankind sharing well-defined characteristics; populations characterized by the frequency with which certain genes recur. I refer of course to the color of the skin and eyes, the type of hair, anthropometric features, and sanguineous group. As the physical appearance or *phenotype* may partly reflect the environment (for instance, the height), the hereditary composition or *genotype* is what matters. Acquired characteristics are not hereditary.[7] In the past it seemed rather easy to categorize mankind by a strictly racial division. The great Swedish naturalist Carl Linné, in his "Systema Naturae," 1738, was the first to classify the Indian (or Amerindian, a

[6] Smith (1966), 232, also argues that it "would be possible to write a fairly adequate history of the people of Colombia strictly in terms of racial succession," that is, "the process by which the members of one race are pushed out of the territory they have been occupying and supplanted by those of another. . . ."

[7] As Soviet biologist Lysenko erroneously believed. Dunn and Dobzhansky (1952) is a good popular introduction to human genetics.

more scholarly word) as a fourth race along with the white, the Negro, and the yellow. But more recent research has revealed that racial differences are much more vague and difficult to establish than scholars used to believe. Today, in fact, no racial classification is generally agreed upon. Racial differences have resulted from mutation, natural selection, and genetic drift (the genetic variations resulting from random crossings in small populations), and have been maintained by geographic isolation. Once isolation has been broken, miscegenation has followed. Therefore it is natural that racial distinctions are vague. But in the remote past miscegenation generally occurred between relative neighbors. Only the geographic discoveries of the fifteenth and sixteenth centuries and developments in navigation made possible large-scale miscegenation between geographically distant human groups. Because they offered attractive conditions for numerous immigrating Europeans accompanied by their Negro slaves, the Americas became the principal scene of this biological process. We still know rather little about mestizaje's strictly biological development in Latin America. Only a few small and scattered human groups have been studied thoroughly. The genetic distribution among the so-called Guayquerí Indians of Margarita Island off Venezuela suggests 46 per cent Caucasoid, 13 per cent Negroid, and 41 per cent Amerindian descent.[8]

How important is miscegenation biologically? It is probably insignificant, for no basic biological differences have yet been found among contemporary races, all of which represent a parallel evolution from man's humble beginnings. Therefore we may say with Juan Comas that, as far as we know, "biologically the mestizaje is neither good nor bad." [9] It is significant that all races, to some extent, have adapted themselves to their environment.[10] Miscegenation may thus form men who are more resistant in an especially difficult environment or against certain diseases.[11] How important is miscegenation psychologically and intellectually? This question has been violently discussed. Many an ingenious test has been tried, particularly in the United States, showing that "colored people" have lagged behind. But the issue is not thereby settled in any way, because it has proved impossible to distinguish clearly between the environment's sociocultural effect and the genetic composition in this respect. At least at the present state of research,

[8] Saldanha (1964), 271–272.
[9] Comas (1944), 24.
[10] For an extraordinary Andean example, see Sacchetti (1964).
[11] See, e.g., Vellard (1956), 89.

4

there is no proof to justify a racial division into intellectually "superior" or "inferior" races. It is likely that what Cicero said is true: "Men differ as to knowledge but are equal in their capacity of learning. There is no race that, led by reason, could not attain virtue." [12]

Nevertheless we know that the categorical opinions expressed on race by pseudoscientists have had much more influence — a nefarious influence, at that — than cautious statements made by serious scholars. I refer to the Nazis in Germany, the Afrikander in South Africa, and the segregationists in the American South, but not to them only. Some Asiatic and African nationalists today seem to be convinced that their own race is innately superior. Pseudoscience has been nurtured by many sources, from Aristotle to Darwin, Count Gobineau, Houston Chamberlain, and Alfred Rosenberg, Hitler's theoretician. The racists have successfully appealed to human envy, ignorance, and stupidity by confusing biological and sociocultural concepts under a veil of mysticism.[13]

Race Mixture and Society

If miscegenation is of such limited interest, what then is its historical significance? Its importance lies in its intimate relationship with two social processes: *acculturation,* the mixture of cultural elements, and *assimilation,* or the absorption of an individual or a people into another culture. In Latin America, miscegenation became an important vehicle in acculturation, and very often racial mixture and cultural mixture coincided. But, as we shall see later, sometimes there was acculturation without miscegenation, or miscegenation without acculturation. In any case we must distinguish clearly between the two. The confusion is frequent in historical literature, and the term "mestizaje" (which should refer only to race mixture), loosely used, is especially responsible for this vagueness and ambiguity.[14]

Unlike miscegenation, acculturation is sometimes very painful and difficult for the individual. The one who finds himself in the middle of

[12] Quoted by Benedict (1959), 96. Shapiro (1953) gives a good summary of miscegenation.

[13] At present, *The Mankind Quarterly* is the mouthpiece of a group of racist intellectuals. Unfortunately, UNESCO and its collaborators, when fighting racism, have also sometimes made use of somewhat simplified arguments. Beckman (1966).

[14] See the remarks of Juan Comas, IPGH (1961), 96. (Bibliographic abbreviations that appear in footnotes throughout this book are spelled out in the Bibliography on pages 153–173 in their alphabetical places.)

this process, whether he is a "mixed blood" or not, risks becoming what has ingeniously been called a "marginal man," a rootless, unstable, uneasy misfit.[15] A racially "pure" person belonging to the elite in one of today's "new" countries may become a marginal man, torn as he is between traditional and external culture. But persons of mixed ancestry probably more frequently have become marginal men. Why? Obviously, the hierarchic classification of human races dictated by European ethnocentricity is the cause. But prior to 1500 differential valorization of human races is hardly noticeable. Admittedly, interracial contacts were also much less frequent. It seems as if Western man was made conscious of racial characteristics, above all, by Renaissance curiosity. Once one became aware of these racial characteristics, there was but a short step to valuation from the point of view of one's own race. But when European colonization of the New World was just beginning, another, clearly medieval, distinction prevailed for some time, that between Christians and heathens. Pagandom provided a convenient excuse for conquest and enslavement, but as the Indians were gradually Christianized, this medieval distinction was soon undermined. Therefore, the distinction between the races in the Americas was derived from the typically colonial dichotomy between conquerors and conquered, masters and servants or slaves. Consequently, miscegenation might itself be conceived as a threat against the established political, economic, and social order. The mulatto as well as the Negro was stigmatized for being a slave or descended from slaves. Another stigma was the illegitimate birth of so many people of mixed ancestry. In this way, many people of color in the Americas became marginal men, rejected by both parental stocks or themselves refusing to join the parental stock considered "inferior."

We must, of course, keep in mind that the contemporary Latin American distinction between "Indians" and others usually reflects a social reality (the Indian's lack of assimilation) and not a racial reality. This is precisely why the word *indígena*, indigenous, one who lives like an Indian, is justly applied here. Though the word "ethnic" is often used merely as a synonym for "racial," sociologists in the United States use it to designate groups characterized by cultural or religious traits, which meaning may render it useful also in Latin American studies. The relationship of the indígenas to others in Latin America is obviously that of a "minority group," a designation applied by American

[15] See, e.g., Stonequist (1937).

6

sociologists to ethnic groups victimized by prejudice and discrimination. In this sense the indígenas, even if numerically they form the majority in a certain region, are a minority group.[16]

It is important also to distinguish clearly between "prejudice" and "discrimination." Ethnic prejudice may be defined as an antipathy based on deficient or inflexible generalizations and directed against a racial, religious, or other group as such and against the members of that group. Sometimes, prejudice is no more than a feeling; sometimes it is expressed in action. The mildest form of action is of course the oral, no matter how vicious the words. Discrimination refuses the members of the group subject to prejudice the equality of treatment that they desire. And segregation is one of the many forms of discrimination devised by human prejudice. But, properly speaking, segregation is only discriminatory insofar as it is imposed against the wishes of a group subject to prejudice.[17]

Social Stratification

To complete this chapter we now present some concepts related to social stratification; that is, the division of society into superposed layers. One may discern three main types of social stratification.[18] First is the *caste* system, a society composed of closed and endogamous groups in which membership is decided by birth. The prototype of this system is, as we know, Hindu India. Second, the *estate* system, a hierarchic society the strata of which are rigidly separated by law and customs and often characterized by their different hereditary relationship to land (as owners, tenants, or serfs). Though social status is generally hereditary, *vertical social mobility* is not altogether excluded. The prototype of this system is to be found in the feudal system of the Middle Ages. Third is the system of *classes*, based mainly on economic differences without legal restrictions on vertical social mobility. In reality societies show easily defined stratifications much less often than forms that are more or less mixed. The evolution of societies has caused the

[16] Wagley and Harris (1958) investigate the Indians of Brazil and Mexico as minority groups.

[17] The classical work on this topic is Allport (1958).

[18] Here I follow Mayer (1955). Sociologists differ a great deal in analyzing and classifying the phenomena related to social stratification. P. Sorokin, for instance, distinguishes between economic, political, and occupational stratification.

emphasis to be shifted from one criterion for social stratification to another. Under the estate system, the individual's *status* or prestige was of paramount importance notwithstanding the permanence of economic differences. In the society of economic classes that slowly took shape in the Western world during the eighteenth and nineteenth centuries, status still is significant but no longer is decisive.

This writer is no friend of the prolific use of learned words and concepts, but if they have to be used, they must be clearly defined. Only then can we use them to clarify our thoughts and prevent confusion. In this book, we are going to follow the historical evolution of two parallel processes in Latin America: mestizaje or miscegenation, and acculturation, with its logical sequel, assimilation. But we cannot confine our historical study of this giant twin process to a very narrow framework. It will be necessary to touch upon the history of Latin American race relations in general in order to grasp the mestizaje's reality and significance.

II

American, Iberian, and African Antecedents

The Indians

Of the three groups that fathered the Latin Americans of today, prior to 1810 practically all the Europeans came from the Iberian Peninsula, whereas the forced immigration of Africans had come to a complete stop around 1850. Each of the three groups was characterized by its heterogeneity.

The first Amerindians arrived via the Straits of Bering about 25,000 B.C., the last waves perhaps 20,000 years later. Anthropologists have abandoned by now their hopes of finding an Amerindian prototype. Some groups are more, others less Mongoloid. What can be noticed among them is a lack of the B blood group, which, on the contrary, is rather common among the Mongoloids of Asia.[1] The thousand generations that have passed since the first migrants arrived have allowed of certain changes in their genetic heritage. The process of adapting to different geographical media also helps to explain the differences between Amerindian peoples. The linguistic diversity is impressive. According to Paul Rivet there are 123 linguistic families; 73 of these in South America are completely different. A recent catalogue lists 260 languages in Mexico and Guatemala. Though the new techniques of

[1] Wolf (1962), 23.

glottochronology permit scholars to study the evolution of this extreme linguistic diversity, no common denominator has yet been found.[2] In fact, there are some similarities between certain South American and Malayo-Polynesian tongues.

By 2500 B.C. or earlier, agriculture was added to the previous economic activities of the Amerindians, i.e., hunting and gathering seeds and roots.[3] By the middle of the first millennium B.C. the first high cultures made their appearance. In response to the challenge of which Arnold Toynbee speaks, they emerged in geographic environments at least superficially adverse, such as the high plateaus and, for the Mayas, the tropical lowland. The population increased as it interacted with the increasingly advanced agriculture in the highlands, comprising irrigation, fertilization, and terrace construction. It is true that the Mayas were able to create their impressive civilization using slash-and-burn agriculture, but the very weakness of this material basis seems to have been responsible for the Maya civilization's decline. Therefore we may venture the generalization that there were, on the one hand, the highlands, with intensive agriculture permitting a dense population, and on the other, the lowlands, where primitive agriculture, carried out by the women, or hunting and gathering permitted only a more or less sparse population. It is true that the lowlands also showed striking contrast between the sedentary or pseudosedentary agriculture of the Guaraníes and the Arawaks and the rudimentary economy of the nomadic tribes, a difference naturally reflected in the relative population densities.

With all due respect to the many sublime and sophisticated expressions of the pre-Columbian cultures and the advanced highland agriculture, we must bear in mind that all these societies were basically inferior to the contemporary European civilization in technology. The absence of iron was one important factor; the absence of the wheel another. And the sociopolitical structure in pre-Columbian civilizations, with varying forms of collectivism and theocracy, reflected more remote stages of development.

In this rapid survey we must briefly touch upon another controversial topic: the extent of pre-Columbian populations in the Americas. Statistical information from the period of the Conquest is not lacking, but its value is lessened by several circumstances. In the first

[2] *Ibid.*, 35ff.
[3] Armillas (1962), 48–52. Cf. Wolf (1962), 50ff.

place, it would have been physically impossible for the Spaniards and Portuguese to count the Indians, unless they had obtained complete control over them. They usually did not do so until years after the first contact, a demographically critical period. Then, Europeans of the pre-industrial age lacked interest in the comprehension for exact figures. Sometimes the invaders used "hundred" or "thousand" as synonyms for "a large crowd" or "a great multitude." In addition, Conquistadors as well as missionaries consciously or unconsciously often exaggerated the number of Indians whom they had defeated or converted. Thus it is obvious that more evidence is needed. One has to estimate the maximum yield of the lands cultivated at the time by the existing techniques, and discount the effect of later erosion or other ecological changes. It is also possible to calculate the manpower needed to construct the archeological monuments that are all that remains of lost civilizations. Eric Wolf estimates that building the Pyramid of the Sun of Teotihuacán (near Mexico City) must have absorbed a labor force of 10,000 for twenty years.[4] Furthermore, it is possible to extrapolate backward, using lists of tributary Indians and other relatively trustworthy documentation from the first half of the sixteenth century. But even having combined these methods, scholars have been very far from reaching any agreement. In the 1920's, Karl Sapper and Herbert Spinden estimated a pre-Columbian population of about 40–50 million, in striking contrast to A. L. Kroeber, who admitted only 8.4 million for the whole of the Americas.[5] In 1945, Angel Rosenblat presented a calculation based mainly on historical sources, according to which the Americas had a population of 13,385,000 in 1492 (4–5 million in Mexico and 2 million in Peru).[6] Rosenblat's figures have become widely known and have been accepted by many historians.

Since 1948, a group of scholars associated with the University of California at Berkeley (historians L. B. Simpson and Woodrow Borah and physiologist S. F. Cook) have been presenting increasingly revolutionary calculations for Central Mexico, obtained with the help of a very sophisticated methodology.[7] According to them, Central Mexico had a population of no fewer than 25 million people on the eve of the

[4] Wolf (1962).

[5] Sapper (1924); Spinden (1928); Kroeber (1939).

[6] Rosenblat (1945; 1954).

[7] Cook and Simpson (1948); Borah and Cook (1963) and other studies by the same authors.

11

Conquest. Even if, as they admit, Mexico therefore was by then over-populated by comparison with the existing resources,[8] so great a figure is hard to accept, from a common-sense point of view, when we remember that the urbanized and industrialized Central Mexico of today has about the same population. Nevertheless, the results obtained by the Berkeley school cannot possibly be ignored and all earlier estimates have been rendered obsolete. It remains to study the rest of the Americas, using similar methods.[9] As it is, calculations of the Inca Empire's population oscillate between 32 million and 3 million.[10] Meanwhile, Borah has ventured to conjecture that there were about 100 million Indians in the New World in 1492.[11] Even if we reduce this figure by two thirds, and it could hardly be less, that would be twice Rosenblat's estimate. We might add that if there were 50 million or more Indians in the New World, the demographic disaster that took place after 1492 is probably without counterpart in the history of mankind.

The Iberians

The Europeans who arrived in the present Latin America prior to 1810, as already mentioned, were almost exclusively Spaniards or Portuguese. The exclusivist Spanish policy was very explicit in this respect. It is true that there were exceptions both in the beginning and toward the end of the colonial period, as exemplified by the German *conquistadores* in Venezuela and by the names of heroes from the wars of emancipation, such as Bernardo O'Higgins and Juan Pueyrredón. But the foreigners, who lived in Latin America illegally or were tolerated by

[8] Borah and Cook (1962). They conclude that the situation would have been disastrous even if the Spaniards had not arrived.

[9] In a recent study of Colombia, Jaramillo Uribe (1964) concludes that there were fewer than 1 million Indians in that region on the eve of the Conquest. The result is in striking contrast to those of the Berkeley school. At the International Congress of Americanists in Argentina in 1966 the Berkeley school was strongly criticized in a paper presented by A. Rosenblat. Some of this criticism was justified, no doubt, but this does not mean that Rosenblat's own calculations deserve to be accepted.

[10] The low calculation by G. Kubler, HSAI, II, 339, the high by Means (1931). If one accepts, as does Harris (1964), 15, that there were 20 million in Central Mexico, then it is obviously inconsistent to calculate only 6 million for the Inca Empire (*ibid.*), 9.

[11] Borah (1962), 179. Partly using other methods, H. F. Dobyns of Cornell University, in an as yet unpublished work, has arrived at a global figure even higher than that of Borah.

the authorities, were hardly numerous enough to deserve demographic attention.[12] On the other hand, the population of the Iberian Peninsula itself was anything but ethnically homogeneous. A long series of peoples had succeeded each other on Iberian soil, merging genetically as well as culturally: Iberians, Celts, Phoenicians, Greeks, Carthaginians, Romans, Visigoths, Jews, Arabs, Berbers, Gypsies, and medieval slaves of different origins. The seven hundred years of coexistence between Moslems and Christians in the Peninsula until the fall of Granada in 1492 witnessed extraordinary acculturation and race mixture. Arabs and Berbers never formed more than a rather small minority in "El Andalus" (Moslem Spain), though the exact proportions are not known. They undoubtedly mixed a great deal with the native population. To speak only of the higher strata, we know that there were blond Caliphs of Córdoba, and that there were Christian princes whose mothers were Moorish. Until the end of the fourteenth century the relations of Jews with both Moslems and Christians were exceptionally open. But from 1391 onward they were subjected to increasingly systematic persecution and segregation. In 1492, the Jews were exiled from Spain, whereas the converted "New Christians" often fell victim to the autos-da-fé of the Inquisition. In 1509, the Jews were also expelled from Portugal. The many *Moriscos* (converted from Islam) who remained, particularly along the Eastern coast of the Peninsula, were expelled in 1609. Though individuals of Moorish or Jewish ancestry were explicitly excluded from emigration to the New World, the Spanish people at the time of Ferdinand and Isabella had already absorbed a great amount of Moorish and Jewish "blood." And, more important, as eloquently demonstrated by Américo Castro, the Moorish and Jewish contributions to acculturation in the Peninsula were profound. This is proved beyond doubt by the frequency of Spanish and Portuguese words of Arab origin, such as those used in navigation, science, and agriculture.

What importance had race mixture and acculturation in the Iberian Peninsula for race relations in the New World? If we are to believe Gilberto Freyre, the Portuguese succeeded as colonizers because of their extraordinary *miscibilidade* (miscibility), acquired over many centuries of social and sexual relationships with the Moors. The invaders, politically and culturally superior, had dark skins, leading to the idealization of the "Moorish enchantress" (*moura encantada*), says Freyre.

[12] A good summary is Konetzke (1965), 65–68, 74.

13

This exalting of the dark woman, coupled with the polygamous Moslem tradition, facilitated and influenced the hybridization that took place in the New World. But the same Freyre has to admit: "It is almost impossible to determine the extent of the infiltration of Moorish blood into the Portuguese, already much Semitic because of remote infiltration of Phenicians and Jews during the advances and retreats of Moslim invasions." In fact, the famous Brazilian writer's theories in this respect are characterized by literary and intuitive imagination rather than by convincing proofs. In any case, Freyre has the common sense to reject another theory elaborated by the Portuguese historian João Lúcio d'Azevedo, who believed that the aristocracy of the country was of "Nordic" origin and the plebeians more or less Africanized. Incidentally, this theory recalls nineteenth-century European racism.[13]

Other students have indicated the undoubted similarities between the Bedouins and the different types of horsemen of the Americas, such as *gauchos* and *llaneros*. They have concluded that North African influence in Spain must be the cause. That may be true, but it is difficult to prove, for the importance of similar environments is difficult to measure. We do know that the cowboys of the fourteenth-century cattle ranges in southern Castile had already acquired many characteristics of their future counterparts in the Indies.[14]

Clearly, we need to know much more about interethnic relations in the Peninsula during Moorish times in order to study their possible influence in the New World. There are obvious facts; the same kind of strange mixture between savage warfare and pacific exchange, including miscegenation, between intolerance and tolerance in interethnic relations, was to be observed in the Americas during the Conquest; this mixture was also characteristic of the Iberian Peninsula during the Middle Ages. Bernal Díaz, the incomparable chronicler of the Conquest of Mexico, speaking of the Spaniards, says on one occasion: ". . . they formed groups of fifteen and twenty and went pillaging the villages, forcing the women and taking cloth and chickens *as if they were in Moorish country* to rob what they found." [15]

In 1956, a specialist on the Iberian background of Latin American history stated: "As far as the history of Iberian population in relation

[13] Freyre (1950), I, 101–103, 385, 390 and *passim*. Azevedo (1930).
[14] E.g., Ornellas (1956); Bishko (1952).
[15] Díaz del Castillo (1955), II, 113.

to overseas colonization is concerned, almost everything remains to be done." [16] This gloomy affirmation is still valid. We know that there were approximately 10 million people in the Peninsula in 1492, about 7 million in Castile, 1 million in Portugal, and 1.5 million in Catalonia-Aragon. It seems as if there was a demographic pressure on available resources, at least in the southern parts.[17] We know very little for certain about the actual emigration overseas. In 1940, the *Archivo General de Indias* in Seville started publishing an ambitious *Catálogo de Pasajeros a Indias*, which contained licenses for departing to the New World from 1509 onward. When it reached the year 1559, the publication had listed 15,480 licenses.[18] As Juan Friede first pointed out, this number is very far from coinciding with the total number of emigrants during that period. Entries are lacking in the *Catálogo* for entire years when other sources show that expeditions sailed to the Indies. During the first decades of the century, many passengers left from ports other than those in Andalusia, unrecorded by the *Catálogo*. Finally, the illegal emigration cannot be ignored, even if it cannot be determined. Total emigration from Spain between 1509 and 1559 may have reached 100,000 instead of the 15,000 recorded in the *Catálogo*.[19] We know even less about the migrations after 1559. A low period during the seventeenth century probably was followed by a period of considerable increase in Spanish emigration during the eighteenth century, but the calculation that appeared in a well-known work some years ago has no scientific value.[20] Of Portuguese emigration we know practically nothing for certain.

If we leave Portugal aside, of what was Spanish migration to the New World composed? Especially in the beginning, the migration was predominantly male. The traditional view has held that Spanish America was settled by single men, in contrast to Anglo-America, which was

[16] Bishko (1956), 63–64.

[17] Friede (1963a). Góngora (1965) gives a thorough, well-balanced account of the socioeconomic factors behind emigration in part of Extremadura. More monographs of this kind are needed.

[18] *Catálogo* (1940–46).

[19] Friede (1951; 1952). On Spanish emigration see also Konetzke (1948; 1952).

[20] I refer to the calculation presented by M. Hernández Sánchez Barba: 52,000 emigrants during the eighteenth century in Vicens Vives (1958), IV, 326. It is based on figures for only three years, chosen arbitrarily, as it seems. On the difficulties in obtaining permission to emigrate around 1800, see Depons (1960), II, 75–77.

settled by families. But even in the early period, from 1509 to 1539, about 10 per cent of the licenses recorded in the *Catálogo* were issued for women, and we know from other sources that there were always women and families among the migrants to Spanish America.[21] The exact percentages on regional distribution sometimes met with in literature are based on the *Catálogo*, the shortcomings of which we have already discussed. The prevalent view that people from Extremadura and Andalusia were predominant is also supported by the evidence provided by language and the life stories of many conquistadores and missionaries. Migration from the Canaries was also important, especially during the eighteenth century, as was that from the Azores to Brazil. Of the migration's social composition we also know very little for certain. Usually it has been taken for granted that *hidalgos*, or lesser nobility, and the younger sons of the aristocrats were predominant. A sample taken by Mario Góngora, who has studied some groups of conquistadores on the Spanish Main, shows, however, that in that migration most of them were peasants and artisans.[22]

The Negroes

The first slaves to cross the Atlantic were the Indians Columbus sent to Spain in 1495.[23] But the slave traffic in the other direction also started very early, during the administration of Governor Ovando in Santo Domingo between 1502 and 1509.[24] The first Negro slaves, already speaking Spanish (*ladinos*), were servants recruited among the many Negro slaves who at the time were kept in Spain as well as in Portugal. In 1565, there were 6,327 Negro slaves in the City of Seville.[25] I remember that I once noticed the negroid features of the people of a village not far from Huelva, and was informed that they were descended from slaves. The stimulus for direct and large-scale slave trade between Africa and the Americas was provided by the exploitation of mines and the establishment of plantations. The Spanish

[21] Konetzke (1945). On the migration of white slaves, see Torre Revello (1927).

[22] Góngora (1962).

[23] Zavala (1948), 98–104, 118–119.

[24] Mellafe (1959), 10–11, 14.

[25] Verlinden (1964?), 35. See also his *magnum opus* (1955), Cortés (1964) and, for Portugal, Correia Lopes (1944). There may have been as many as 10,000 slaves in Lisbon during the latter half of the sixteenth century.

16

Crown granted the first license for exporting slaves to the New World in 1518. The license implied delivery of 4,000 slaves over eight years. In 1528, the Crown granted the first monopoly or *asiento* in the slave trade. Since Spain did not possess any territories along the African coast, the asientos were usually held by foreign interests. A long series of asientos concluded with foreign contractors or enterprises culminated in the famous British "South Sea Company" asiento, which, with some interruptions, lasted from 1713 to 1750. It concerned the annual export to Spanish America of 4,800 *piezas de Indias*, the usual unit for measuring the human merchandise. One pieza corresponded to one male slave in good condition; a couple of minors in poor shape might also be lumped together to form one pieza. During the latter half of the eighteenth century, the slave trade was liberalized (in the economic sense) to make greater quantities available. Portuguese possessions in Africa, particularly Angola, permitted a direct slave trade with Brazil without relying on foreign enterprises. We know rather little about the extent of the slave imports into Brazil. As far as Spanish America is concerned, it is not enough to add the numbers contained in the licenses to get an idea about the traffic. Often, the slavers did not supply as many slaves as the licenses specified that they could and, on the other hand, illegal slave trade was probably often as important as the legal trade. A careful study made by an Argentine scholar shows that about 30,000 Negroes were imported legally via Buenos Aires between 1742 and 1806. In addition, many were imported as contraband, but the total is unknown.[26] A recent study on Venezuela calculates that the total importation during the colonial period was 121,168 slaves, and that 70,513 were brought in during the eighteenth century.[27] It is clear that the total imported into Brazil over 450 years must be estimated in millions, but the destruction of records relating to slavery after the abolition in 1888 has made the reconstruction almost impossible. A guess by an authoritative historian gives a total of some 4 million (up to 1850),[28] whereas the total for Spanish America may have reached 3 million. To try to calculate this enormous migration from the African side is probably even more hazardous.

[26] Scheuss de Studer (1958).

[27] Brito Figueroa (1963), 137. Other works on the importing of slaves to Spanish America: Scelle (1906); Aguirre Beltrán (1946); Otte and Ruíz Burruecos (1963); Mellafe (1959; 1965).

[28] Buarque de Hollanda (1960), 191. According to Mauro (1960), 180, 400,000 slaves were introduced to Brazil from 1570 to 1670.

Another author recently conjectured that the slave trade cost Africa 50 million people, but the figure seems inflated.[29] Nevertheless, the margin between export and import figures must have been considerable because of the mortality aboard the slavers, terribly high on the whole, a result of bad treatment, dysentery, and other diseases. The impression I received when I studied the records of the British Asiento agency in Buenos Aires for the beginning of the eighteenth century was that a loss of between 15 and 20 per cent of the human cargo was considered normal.

Where did the slaves come from? Their origin varied a great deal, but by far the majority came from the West African coast between the Senegal River in the north (with the Portuguese strongholds of Cacheu and Bissau) and Portuguese Angola in the south. This region comprised several highly stratified societies, rather advanced in material civilization and cultural and spiritual life. The later decline, partly a result of the slave trade itself, should not obscure the greatness of the Yoruba Kingdom of Oyo, of the Kingdoms of Dahomey, Benin, and Congo. In the northern parts of the region Moslem influence was also important. The slaves were generally classified according to the port of departure. Since they came from the interior, these denominations say little about their real origin.[30] Therefore, modern anthropologists have had to study the question mainly on the basis of the cultural elements that the slaves brought to the New World.[31] This is not easy, for every one of the slavers picked up his cargos in different ports. After their arrival in the New World the slaves were also scattered in all directions. Every plantation housed slaves from a great many different tribes. The lack of a common language forced the slaves to adopt the language of their masters, an important step in the forced acculturation to which they were subjected. Furthermore, the very conditions of their passage and their existence as slaves made it impossible for them to bring any artifacts and other property to the New World. Under these adverse conditions, it is surprising that, after all, the slaves were able to exert such influence as they did upon folk religion, language, music, dances, and agriculture of the Americas. If the form of migration and treatment had been somewhat more humane, there can be no doubt

[29] Davidson (1961), 87–88.

[30] King (1943) shows, however, that patterns of cicatrices on the bodies of Negroes mentioned in bills of sale, etc., may be used to trace the tribal origin of the slaves.

[31] I refer, e.g., to the well-known studies of Melville Herskovits.

18

that their contribution would have been much more important. As it was, the professional skill of many African blacksmiths and other artisans among the slaves was wasted by their masters, who wanted only brute, strong, field hands. The fact that the Negro proved physically superior to the Indian worker was not only due to his previous experience of forced labor. The Africans had acquired resistance against many of the diseases that the white man brought to the New World, with such devastating results. Finally, the selection made by slave traders, based on physical fitness and the merciless weeding out of all weaker slaves during the voyage, made the Negro immigrants a biological elite.[32]

As we have seen, all factors in the demographic equation are very uncertain. There can be no doubt, however, that for more than a century after the Discovery, Amerindians formed by far the largest group in the populations of present Latin America. It is also without question that the material, military, technological, and also cultural superiority of the Europeans allowed them to dictate the evolution in the so-called New World. The African contribution to acculturation, as mentioned above, was less than it could have been because of the peculiar conditions of their migration.

[32] Harris (1964), 14–16.

Zambo chieftains from Esmeraldas (in present-day Ecuador), who visited Quito in 1599. Notice the Spanish dress and Indian ornaments worn by these descendants of shipwrecked Negro slaves whom the Spaniards were unable to subdue. Courtesy of Museo de América, Madrid.

III

First Meeting of the Races in the Americas

The Conquest of Women

When they went ashore, Columbus and his men found that often the Indians of the Antilles tried to hide their women from the white strangers. On other occasions the Indian women showed themselves and were even importune in their admiration for the newcomers. Naturally enough, the discoverers thought that the first attitude was due to the jealousy of the Indian husbands, whereas the women, of course, were only expressing their love. Such a romantic interpretation of the first meeting of the races can also be found in the accounts of contemporary chroniclers and later historians. But in 1924 a Spanish historian made the sobering observation that the Indian attitudes would be better explained by their animist belief. At first they had to resist the alien spirits. When this was no longer possible, they had to surrender entirely. In addition, the Arawaks were not aware of any relationship between copulation and pregnancy. The latter was explained merely in an animistic way.[1] However true this may be, perhaps the boldness of the alien spirits at last succeeded in arousing the jealousy of the Indian husbands — when Columbus returned to Hispaniola on his second voyage, he found that the men he had left there had been killed. The Indians explained, an eyewitness reports, that one of the

[1] Maldonado de Guevara (1924); Columbus (1960), 111.

21

Spaniards "had taken three women to himself, and another four; from whence we drew the inference that jealousy was the cause of the misfortune that had occurred." [2]

From the very beginning, Spanish and Portuguese eyewitnesses and chroniclers devoted enthusiastic accounts to the beauty of the Indian girls. Also, a tough German mercenary, Ulrich Schmidel, who took part in the conquest of Río de la Plata, sounds inspired when talking about the Jarayes women: "Very handsome and great lovers, affectionate and with ardent bodies, in my opinion." [3] I would be the last to deny that such expressions in the otherwise not overly romantic chronicles might sometimes be sincere and based on experience. In fact, the female type of the forest tribes is rather close to the feminine ideal in Europe during the Renaissance and later. But I suspect that the sixteenth-century authors sometimes dwelt on the beauty and enchantment of the Indian women in order to satisfy the literary taste of the times. Therefore there is little reason to take these accounts very seriously, or to refer to them, as some historians do, as explaining the rapidity and character of the process of race mixture. Above all it would, as I see it, be absurd to consider them an evidence of a lack of prejudice on the part of the conquistadores. The basic explanation of the rapidity with which race mixture proceeded after the first contact is undoubtedly to be found in the lack of white women at the time of the first expeditions, and the months of abstention during the passage. The satisfaction of a natural instinct should not be confused with social and esthetic attitudes. In fact, the seventeenth-century Dutch did not hesitate to mix with the Bushmen of South Africa, probably the ugliest females to be found in the world, from the European point of view. [4]

In a way, the Spanish Conquest of the Americas was a conquest of women. The Spaniards obtained the Indian girls both by force and by peaceful means. The seizure of women was simply one element in the general enslavement of Indians that took place in the New World during the first decades of the sixteenth century. Indian slavery was finally

[2] Columbus (1961), 51.

[3] Schmidel (1938), 113.

[4] The account by Pérez de Barradas (1948) is romantic and uncritical. Rosenblat (1954), II, also attributes mestizaje partly to a supposed lack of racial prejudice on the part of Spaniards and Portuguese. Even Konetzke (1946), 28ff., does not seem critical enough in this respect. Cautious reservation made by Salas (1960), 24–25.

prohibited categorically in the New Laws of 1542. It then gradually disappeared, at least in most areas of Spanish America.[5] But Schmidel tells us about a campaign in Gran Chaco in 1547 that rendered him no fewer than fifty slaves: men, women, and children.[6] In Chile, where the Spaniards faced the stubborn resistance of the warlike Araucanos, the enslavement of the Indians, including that of their women, was once again made legal in 1608.[7] Bernal Díaz, that remarkable eyewitness of the conquest of Mexico, presents a lively account of the actual enslavement of women. Cortés had decided that all the slaves taken by the soldiers should be branded, so that the Royal fifth (the Crown's share) and his own share of the human booty could be taken. When the soldiers returned the following day to recover the remaining slaves, they discovered to their dismay that Cortés and his officers had "hidden and taken away the best looking slaves so that there was not a single pretty one left. The ones we received were old and ugly. There was much grumbling against Cortés on this account. . . ."[8] Military campaigns have no doubt always been accompanied by rape and other brutalities against the defenseless. It seems, however, that violence possesses special characteristics during warfare between peoples representing widely different civilizations. Critical, then, is the lack of common ethical norms,[9] as in the wars between Christians and Moslems in the Iberian Peninsula, and also during the Conquest of the Americas.

Perhaps the element of violent rape should not be overemphasized. Though prematrimonial virginity was highly considered by certain tribes, the opposite was true among others. Probably the Indian women very often docilely complied with the conquistadores' desires.[10]

The Spaniards also obtained women in the form of gifts and as tokens of friendship from the Indian *caciques*. This kind of hospitality has existed in many other environments and ages. Bernal Díaz tells us how the Cacique Xicotenga offered Cortés his virgin daughter and four other pretty girls to his captains. Similar episodes abound in the chronicles of the times.[11] From Paraguay, Rui Díaz de Guzmán reports that the Guaraní caciques considered the gift of women to be an

[5] The best study of Indian slavery is Konetzke (1949).
[6] Quoted by Konetzke (1946), 19.
[7] Jara (1960), 205–207.
[8] Díaz del Castillo (1955), I, 428.
[9] Frazier (1957), 46.
[10] Gutiérrez de Pineda (1963), I, 67ff.
[11] Díaz del Castillo (1955), I, 222.

excellent means of allying themselves with the Spaniards. "They called all of them brothers-in-law. This is the origin of the existing custom of calling the Indians entrusted to you *Tobayá* which means brother-in-law. And it so happened that the Spaniards had many sons and daughters with the Indian women they received." [12] Once confirmed by the gift of women, the alliances between Spaniards and Indians were likely to be strong and lasting. This could very well be of greatest importance for the success of a small group of conquistadores. As Inca Garcilaso de la Vega puts it, "as soon as the Indians saw that a woman had been begotten by a Spaniard, all the kinsfolk rallied to pay homage to the Spaniard as their idol and to serve him because they were now related to him. Such Indians were of great help during the Conquest of the Indies." [13]

Another way of obtaining women was provided by the *encomienda*, the famous institution by which Indians were distributed among Spaniards who were granted their tribute. In his turn, the recipient of an encomienda was supposed to protect and civilize his Indians and see to it that they were Christianized. At least until the New Laws (1542), the Indians usually paid their tributes to the *encomendero* in days of work. It is not surprising that the encomenderos often asked for female domestic servants. As Bishop Juan de Zumárraga of Mexico observed, in his well-known letter to Emperor Charles in 1529, such servants were used as concubines more often than not. Near Cuenca in present Ecuador, Cieza de León reports, the Indians sent their wives and daughters to carry the Spaniards' luggage, while they stayed at home. The chronicler remarks that these women were "beautiful, and not a little lascivious, and fond of the Spaniards." [14] It also happened that the Indians paid their tribute in slaves, men or women. Slavery already existed among many Indian tribes on different cultural levels. The Indians also occasionally sold female slaves to the Spaniards. This traffic was prohibited by the New Laws.[15]

However the Spaniard and the Portuguese of the early sixteenth century had obtained them, by force, purchase, or gift, he lived surrounded by Indian women. Sometimes they were his slaves or the kind of serfs called *naborías* in the Caribbean and *yanaconas* in Peru; some-

[12] Quoted by Konetzke (1946), 24–25.
[13] Quoted by Varallanos (1962), 45.
[14] Marshall (1939), 173; Cieza de León (1945), 145.
[15] *Recopilación*, VI-I-6. See also Díaz del Castillo (1955), II, 387–388.

times they were, theoretically, free servants. This way of life often produced the impression of a real harem, though some accounts of contemporary observers seem exaggerated, perhaps because they were shocked or too enthusiastic. We should not take as a statistically verified fact the report that in Paraguay, called the Paradise of Mohammed, every Spaniard had an average of twenty to thirty women.[16]

The Church, of course, by no means approved of this situation, but it was certainly not easy to do anything about it. The Bishop of Santo Domingo wrote to the Emperor in 1529 that when his Spanish parishioners were living in sin the concubines were their own Indian servants "and nothing can be found out about it." Furthermore, the results of such unions were often born in faraway places. As another report from Santo Domingo during the same period put it: "there are a great many mestizos here, sons of Spaniards and Indian women who are usually born in *estancias* and uninhabited places." [17] The civil authorities during the Conquest were often satisfied with having the Indian women baptized prior to coition. Thus, the commander of an expedition in Cartagena in 1538 was instructed that he should see to it that "no soldier slept with any Indian who was not a Christian." [18] The conquistadores themselves seem to have taken the reproaches for being promiscuous very lightly, whether they were aware of fulfilling a "civilizing" mission or not. Accused by the Inquisition of a great many blasphemous utterances, the old conquistador Francisco de Aguirre, governor of Tucumán, confessed among other things to having declared that "the service rendered to God in producing mestizos is greater than the sin committed by the same act." [19]

Concubinage and Intermarriage

There can be no doubt that casual intercourse and concubinage accounted for most of the crossing during the Conquest.[20] And polygyny was more than frequent. But it should not be forgotten that marriage

[16] As does, e.g., Salas (1960), 189ff.

[17] Quoted by Konetzke (1946), 22–23; for Brazil, see Nóbrega (1955), *passim*.

[18] Gutiérrez de Pineda (1963), I, 183; the same custom reported from Brazil by Nóbrega (1955), 30–31.

[19] Medina (1952), 85.

[20] The assertion of Ots Capdequí (1957), 80, that most Spanish-Indian concubinages ended in marriage, seems to be completely groundless.

also brought about race mixture. Intermarriage was explicitly permitted by the monarch in 1501. Two years later Governor Ovando of Santo Domingo was instructed to see to it that "some Christians [i.e., Spaniards] marry some Indian women and some Christian women marry some Indian men, so that both parties can communicate and teach each other and the Indians become men and women of reason." We shall discuss this decree in its legal context later. Here, we are interested in how such a policy was received in the American environment. The colonial authorities were far from enthusiastic about it, but there were always some churchmen around who put pressure on them to permit or even promote intermarriage. Spanish-Indian couples living in concubinage should be persuaded to marry. According to a chronicler, Governor Ovando ordered the Spaniards in Santo Domingo either to marry their Indian partners or to part company: "In order not to lose their authority over the Indian women and their services they married them." [21] But even with such methods rather little was achieved. A census taken in Santo Domingo in 1514 revealed that only 171 of the 689 Spaniards living there were married. The wives of 107 were Spanish (5 of them having been left behind in Spain), and only 64 were natives. Those married to Indian women usually belonged to the lowest social stratum.[22] The policy of the Crown also vacillated a great deal with regard to intermarriage. By its orders, numbers of white female slaves were sent to the Indies. The Royal decree of 1514 explained that the very lack of women there was such that it had caused some Spaniards to marry Indian women, "people far from possessing reason." [23] And many Spaniards preferred to marry a white prostitute rather than a native woman. This is why Cervantes called the Americas the "great lure of licentious women." [24] As soon as Spanish women were available, the Spaniards were likely to reject their Indian spouses or favorites. This also happened to "princesses," such as the mother of Inca Garcilaso de la Vega. The famous writer himself sadly states: "In Peru there have been few who have married in order to legitimize their natural offspring enabling them to inherit." [25]

It seems fair to draw two conclusions on the basis of what we know

[21] *CDHFS*, I, 12–13; Konetzke (1946), 215–216.
[22] Konetzke (1946), 218.
[23] Konetzke (1946), 235.
[24] Cervantes de Saavedra (1949), 902.
[25] Vega (1959), I:2, ch. I.

about race mixture during the Conquest. In the first place, the color of the sexual partner was of no importance, as well stated by Juan de Carvajal, a conquistador of Venezuela. When accused of promiscuity he flatly replied: "No one in these parts who has a homestead can live without women, Spanish or Indian." [26] Second, it is obvious that the Spaniards preferred to marry Spanish women, above all, probably because of their desire to provide their descendants with a good lineage.

To the Indian women, association with the conquistadores offered many advantages, even though they were not allowed to marry. But many seem to have become aware of their inferiority to their white rivals. Chronicler Gonzalo Fernández de Oviedo tells a pathetic story of how Indian girls tried to bleach their skin. The Indian women could hope that the children they had with the whites would be accepted as free "Spaniards." [27]

In the beginning, such expectations seemed to be fulfilled. As a rule, the first generation of mestizos was accepted as "Spaniards." This is easy to understand for mestizos born in marriage, but, as we have pointed out, these were not at all frequent. On the other hand, during this early period many mestizos were recognized by their fathers. The process of legitimization seems to have been frequently used at this time both in Spain and Portugal.[28] A very tolerant attitude, indeed, was that of a certain Diego de Ocaña in sixteenth-century New Spain. In his will he confesses that the Indian servant Antonica had been his mistress. Since she also lived with an Indian, however, he did not know for sure who was the father of her child, even if the color made it likely that it was Diego. Be this as it may, he found he had better recognize the child and ask his legitimate children to instruct him and to take good care of him.[29] In another will, that of Domingo Martínez de Irala, a famed conquistador of Paraguay, the list of children sired with seven Indian women comprises three boys and six girls. Whereas six of the mothers were servants of Irala himself, the seventh was "the servant of Diego de Villalpando." Irala had married his daughters to other conquistadores, providing them with the best possible dowry, he declares.[30]

[26] Friede (1961), 405.
[27] Quoted by Salas (1960), 57.
[28] Gutiérrez de Pineda (1963), I, 160–161.
[29] Priestley (1929), 111–112.
[30] Lafuente Machain (1939), 560–561.

The Early Mestizos

Mestizos of this accepted and well-treated category must, as a rule, have felt strong solidarity with the paternal group. In the beginning, mestizo sons were even able to inherit the grant of an encomienda from their Spanish fathers.[31] And the first generation of mestizos took an active part in the last stages of the Conquest. In the River Plate region it was Juan de Garay and his fellow mestizos from Asunción who founded Santa Fé and, finally, Buenos Aires in 1580. In Chile the mestizos were active in the struggles against the Araucanos. In an interesting letter from the governor of Chile to the king in 1585, the former acknowledges receipt of a royal decree restricting the rights of the mestizos. Barely able to suppress his anger, the governor refers to the fact that there are 150 mestizos in the army, most of them sons of the conquistadores. Without them Chile would have been lost, he exclaims: "I should pray to God that there were as many good people among those sent to us from Spain as there are among those Mestizos." [32] In Brazil, it is well known that two shipwrecked Portuguese, "Caramurú" and João Ramalho, with their numerous progeny, helped Governor Tomé de Souza to found the settlements of Baía and São Vicente respectively. The Governor wrote to the king that Ramalho had so many children that he did not dare to put down the number. "Caramurú," for his part, is said to have had at least sixty. However savage and primitive were these Brazilian mestizos ("mamelucos," as they were called), the future explorers of the inland, they obviously remained loyal to the cause of their fathers.[33]

But there were exceptions from the general solidarity of the early mestizos with the paternal group. Some mestizos of the first generation chose to stay with the maternal group or, later in life, came to join it. Most of the "Spanish deserters" who went over to the Araucanos in Chile were probably mestizos. But this phenomenon was not confined to mestizos. Quite a few native Spaniards, some of them involved in shipwreck or captivity, also switched sides, and were assimilated with the Indians. As distinguished from "Caramurú" and Ramalho, some could not revive their original loyalty even by direct contact with com-

[31] Ots Capdequí (1957), 125–126.
[32] *CDIHCh*, III, 268/269. (See Bibliography, pp. 153–173 for full titles.)
[33] On Ramalho see also Nóbrega (1955), 183–184.

28

patriots later on. Thus we have the pathetic Francisco Martín, a member of an expedition of conquest in Venezuela, who "went native" after almost incredible adventures and hardships. Years later he was found by a group of compatriots and was forced to return to "civilization" with them. He soon fled to join his Indian tribe and family but was fetched away for a second time and exiled to New Granada. Chronicler Fernández de Oviedo says that "his love for the wife and children he had in captivity was such that he lamented and wept for them. The Indian ceremonies and customs were also so deeply ingrained in him that by carelessness he sometimes made use of them among Spaniards." [34] Another interesting story is that of the two Spaniards, Jaime Aguilar and Gonzalo Guerrero, who had been taken prisoner in Campeche. When Cortés arrived at Cozumel years later he got to know about them, and forwarded to Aguilar the ransom required to set both of them free. Aguilar, who had come to be more than happy, went to Guerrero to break the news. But the latter replied: "Brother Aguilar, I am married and have three children, and they look on me as a *Cacique* here, and a captain in time of war. Go, and God's blessing be with you. But my face is tattooed and my ears are pierced. What would the Spaniards say if they saw me like this? And look how handsome these children of mine are. . . ." And Guerrero's wife angrily added, storyteller Bernal Díaz says: "Why has this slave come here to call my husband away? Go off with you, and let us have no more of your talk." [35] As an example of acculturation and assimilation, Aguilar was the "misfit," the man incapable of assimilation, whereas Guerrero had been successful in assimilating. In fact, the poor sailor had climbed the social ladder, becoming chieftain and captain of war.

To return to the mestizos of the first generation, we have seen that, obviously, most were absorbed by the paternal group, whereas others joined the Indians. Certainly there were also those who led a marginal existence between the two groups without being accepted by either. But this phenomenon was to occur on a large scale only later on. It is a simple sociological fact that persons of mixed origin tend to be absorbed by either parental group when they are few in number. When they are numerous, though, they are likely to form a group of their own.[36]

[34] Friede (1961), 198–202; Friede (1965), 33–46.
[35] Díaz del Castillo (1955), I, 98.
[36] UNESCO (1956), 315.

The Negro and Early Race Mixture

The Conquest witnessed the beginning of an extensive process of crossing between Caucasoid and Amerindian. Ever since the early years of the sixteenth century, the Negroid element was present, too, though in small numbers.

The first Negroes who appeared in the Indies were Hispanicized *ladinos*, who accompanied their masters as slaves or free servants all the way from Spain. Practically all the conquistador leaders and higher functionaries were able to obtain licenses to bring some slaves with them. Many slaves took an active part in the Conquest; some obtained their freedom in that way.[37] There were also some female Negro slaves around. We know, for instance, that Diego de Almagro Senior set his Negro slave Margarita free. Years later this lady endowed a *capellanía* or pious foundation in 1553 in order to honor and perpetuate the name of the Almagros and that of "other gentlemen and friends of mine who accompanied my master during the expedition that we made to the provinces of Chile." [38] In the open society of the Conquest, it seems that similar spectacular social ascents among the Negroes took place now and then. Many Negro slaves were placed as foremen, *calpisques*, by the encomenderos in the villages of their Indians. The Negroes were urged to find an outlet in racial mixture by the same basic factor that was instrumental among the Europeans: the lack of due proportion between the sexes. Perhaps there were as many as three times as many men as there were women among the Negroes brought to the Indies; the ratio may have been even more unequal. At the same time, the slave status often was a severe handicap in their pursuit of sexual satisfaction. The vigorous efforts that they had to make thus earned the Negroes a reputation for being "boundlessly voluptuous." Logically, their partners were usually Indian women. In fact, it seems as if many Indian women preferred them to their own husbands.[39] Leaving aside possible sexual or psychological factors, this may also have a social explanation. Despite their legal slave status the Negroes,

[37] Mellafe (1964), 22–27; Aguirre Beltrán (1946), Ch. XI–XIV.
[38] Mellafe (1959), 45.
[39] See, e.g., a letter from the viceroy of New Spain to the king in 1574, *CInd*, 299.

by being associated with the Spanish conquerors, automatically came to occupy a position superior to that of the vanquished Indians. There can be no doubt that the Afro-Indian unions during this period almost always took place outside wedlock, being usually of a casual character.

Demographic Disaster

We can be rather sure that the relatively small groups of Europeans and Africans who arrived in the Indies during the first half of the sixteenth century carried on miscegenation as extensively as was feasible, and the opportunities were certainly present. Since most of the offspring joined their fathers and the other Europeans, this dynamic biological activity also opened the way for acculturation and assimilation into the Western civilization. But the advance of the mestizaje during the Conquest would have been much less conspicuous if the Indian masses had remained as numerous as they evidently were prior to contact with the Europeans. In order to assess the importance of the mestizaje during the sixteenth century, we must see it against the background of the terribly rapid decline in the Indian populations.

Even the very cautious calculations made by Angel Rosenblat imply that the aboriginal population of the Americas was reduced from 13.3 million to 10.8 million between 1492 and 1570. As for the whites, Negroes, and mixed population, Rosenblat assesses their number as no more than 3.5 per cent of the population in 1570 (19 per cent in 1650).[40] The very detailed calculations prepared by the Berkeley school team of historians and demographers show an infinitely more dramatic curve than that of Rosenblat for Central Mexico:

1519	25,200,000
1532	16,800,000
1548	6,300,000
1568	2,650,000
1580	1,900,000
1595	1,375,000
1605	1,075,000

Even though the figure for 1519 is admittedly hypothetical (based on an average of 4.5 persons per family), the following figures, especially from 1568 onward, seem to be better documented, based as they

[40] Rosenblat (1954), I, 88, 102.

31

are, above all, on fiscal records.[41] At the same time, Woodrow Borah, one of these scholars, thinks that the so-called Spanish population in the same region increased from about 57,000 in 1570 to 114,000 in 1646. Another American scholar, Henry Dobyns, suggests that it is most likely that the Central Andean Zone underwent a similar disastrous demographic decline, but the topic remains to be studied with serious methods.[42] Scattered evidence from other parts of the Americas also indicates a sharp downward trend after "contact." An investigation of the Quimbaya tribe in present Colombia shows that the number of Indians liable to tribute dropped from 15,000 in 1539 to only 69 in 1628.[43] The demographic disaster was obviously the keynote of sixteenth-century Latin American history, though our knowledge so far is very incomplete. "Like the baroque altars soon to arise in the colony, the splendor and wealth of the new possessions but covered a grinning skull," as Eric Wolf expresses this tragic reality.[44]

The primary causes of the demographic decline were the imported diseases: smallpox, typhus, measles, and influenza. Isolated from the rest of the world as they had been, the Amerindians had developed no resistance at all against these diseases. Smallpox, introduced into Mexico by a sick Negro participant of Narváez' expedition in 1520, spread havoc among the Indians not yet reached by the Spaniards. In a similar way European diseases reached Peru in the 1520's, ahead of the conquistadores themselves. The striking discrepancy between the demographic figures for New Spain in 1568 and 1580 resulted from the epidemic of *matlalzáhuatl*, probably a variety of typhoid. Malaria, trachoma, and yellow fever seem to have been brought to the Americas from Africa by Negro slaves, who themselves often fell victims to dysentery.[45]

In attributing the horrible mortality primarily to these imported diseases I am not ignoring the fact that great numbers of Indians were victims of violence and cruel treatment inflicted by the conquistadores.

[41] Borah (1951), 18 and *passim*; Cook and Borah (1960) and other studies by these two scholars. Whereas Borah places the demographic nadir around 1650, Miranda (1962), on the basis of additional sources, suggests that demographic recovery in Central Mexico set in between 1620 and 1630. When tracing the demographic evolution of Chile, 1540–1620, Mellafe (1959), 212–226, places the nadir around 1600.

[42] Dobyns (1963).

[43] Friede (1963), 253–254.

[44] Wolf (1962), 195.

[45] Ashburn (1947).

But I think it is obvious that quantitatively such causes were infinitely less important. We cannot reasonably attribute casualties as heavy as might be expected in atomic war to sixteenth-century warfare techniques.

Here we must also say a few words about one of the venereal diseases, a subject intimately related to the mestizaje. The specialists agree that syphilis made its first, well-documented appearance during the siege of Naples by the French in 1495. But they disagree on its origin. Was it brought from the New World with Columbus' sailors or was it, on the contrary, of Old World origin? The problem is perhaps impossible to settle because of the vagueness of medieval diagnostics and the confusion with other venereal diseases in Europe and Asia.[46] Be this as it may, syphilis and the other venereal diseases spread very rapidly in the New World in the wake of the mestizaje. Stressing the rapidity of this process in Brazil, sociologist Gilberto Freyre has coined the word "syphilization," as a kind of counterpart to "civilization." [47]

[46] The opposite views are represented by Ashburn (1947), 186ff., and Wolf (1962), 196, 283.
[47] Freyre (1950), I, 161–162.

De Eſpañol,é India,Meſtizo.

A Spaniard, his Indian wife, **and their** mestizo son; an eighteenth-century painting. Courtesy of Museo de América, Madrid.

IV

Racial Policies of State and Church in Colonial Times

Law and Intermarriage in Spanish America

In spite of the many similarities between the "racial" policies of Spain and Portugal in America, a clear distinction must be made. Let us start with Spain.

Several factors determined the approach of the Spanish Crown to social policy and legislation. First, we must notice the intimate relationship between state and Church established on the basis of royal patronage. Within this institutional framework, the priests were a very influential pressure group, whose influence on royal policy was especially great during the sixteenth century. Second, we have to bear in mind the extraordinary ambitions of the state during the Age of Mercantilism, and its desire to regulate every part of society by means of legislation, somewhat in the manner of the socialist welfare state of the twentieth century. Third, the extremely casuistic character of the legislation enacted for Spanish America should be remembered. This legislation was meant merely to apply and supplement the principles adopted by the laws of the *Siete Partidas* of medieval Castile. Thus, Spanish American legislation was formed by a series of administrative decisions arrived at in certain cases and with regard to local jurisdictions. Nevertheless, such decisions sometimes were given the character of general laws. In 1680, Spanish American law was codified in the famous *Recopilación de Leyes de los Reinos de las Indias*. Since the individual laws usually had their origin in demands made by some interested party in Spanish America, there were, of course, frequent contradictions within the legislation and sometimes principles were clouded by the many exceptions that were permitted. Finally, in order to understand Spanish American law we must keep in mind (though this is not often done) that legislation continued to develop for not less than three hundred years. During this long period, changes affected both form and content. Therefore, the chronological determination is imperative when dealing with Spanish American colonial law.

Intermarriage holds a key position within the "racial" policy of the Spanish Crown. Canonical law considered different religions an obstacle to marriage. In addition, the "purity of the blood" concept, as developed from the fifteenth century onward, also opposed marriage with the "New Christians," the converted Jews. On the other hand, it does not seem that there were any obstacles to intermarriage between Spaniards and native Guanche women in the Canaries.[1] Two other canonical precepts should be remembered: the liberty of the individual to contract marriage as he wished, within clearly defined limits, and the obligation that consorts live together.

This last principle was put to a severe test by the colonization of the New World. Many Spaniards departed for the Indies, leaving their wives in Spain. The Crown let them choose between returning to their wives or sending for their wives to join them in the New World. But these pious intentions proved difficult to carry out. Instead, the negligent husbands often were able to obtain the legalization of an abnormal situation by purchase. This procedure was called *composición*, an all too flexible legal device that was later used to solve many other legal and administrative dilemmas.[2] Another phenomenon was the separation of Indian husbands from their wives by the different forms of forced labor. In this case as well, the legislator tried to remedy a canonically unsatisfactory situation, without much success. In 1528 it was decreed illegal to keep an Indian woman separated from her husband, even if she desired it herself.[3] In the royal instructions for Gov-

---

[1] Sicroff (1960). On the Guanches, Konetzke (1946), 119; Zavala (1948), 87, 91.
[2] Haring (1963), 197.
[3] Ots Capdequí (1957), 95.

ernor Ovando in 1501 it had been laid down that Indian women should not be retained against their wishes. It was added that if Spaniards wanted to marry Indian girls, "this had to be done voluntarily on both sides and not forcibly." [4] Two years later, Ovando, as already mentioned, was instructed to arrange a number of mixed marriages. This instruction has been cited as a proof that the Crown really promoted intermarriage and the fusion of races. I am inclined to agree with Richard Konetzke, however, in believing that the orders received by Ovando were merely another of the social experiments characteristic of the early sixteenth century in the New World. In fact, white female slaves were sent to the Indies precisely in order to avoid unions with the Indians, "people who are far from possessing reason," in the words of the royal decree. It is true that two years later, in 1514, the liberty for Spaniards to marry Indians was once again and definitely decreed, but this only meant that the canonical rule was applied to the liberty of marriage. It was not intended to promote intermarriage.[5]

Only two kinds of intermarriage seem to have been actively promoted by the Crown. In 1516, Cardinal Cisneros, as Regent of Castile, issued instructions for the three Hieronimite friars who had been placed in charge of the government in the Indies. One of the instructions stressed that the Spaniards ought to marry the daughters of the caciques when they were "the successors of their fathers in the absence of sons . . . because in that way all the caciques would soon be Spaniards." [6] What the Cardinal did not know was that inheritance among the tribes of the Caribbean, more often than not, was transmitted on the maternal side. The Indian systems of kinship often caused bewilderment and misunderstanding among the Spaniards. In any case, it seems that there were quite a number of intermarriages of this category.[7] The other instance of at least indirect promotion of intermarriage was that of the encomenderos. In 1539, they were ordered to marry within three years or, if already married but living alone, to send for their wives from Spain under penalty of losing their encomiendas.[8]

[4] CDFS, I, 5.
[5] Konetzke (1946), 216; Torre Revello (1927).
[6] CDFS, I, 64.
[7] Gutiérrez de Pineda (1963), 188–190 and *passim*. Missionary Gumilla (1740), 86, observes that "Spanish" mothers did not object to marriage between a son and mestizo or Indian girls "especially if he married the daughter of some cacique."
[8] CDFS, I, 193. Cf. 187 and Levillier (1922), lxvii.

This measure seems to have led to occasional formalizations of unions with Indian women. A chronicler in Peru states that the encomenderos now "married their Indian concubines who were of noble origin." [9] But the obligation that encomenderos marry, imposed for moralistic considerations, implies, we repeat, only an indirect promotion of intermarriage.

On the other hand, the Crown on the whole opposed intermarriage with the African element. One of the reasons for this attitude was that slaves were to be prevented from obtaining freedom for their children, or even for themselves, in this way. By analogy with the conditions of servitude in medieval Castile, this might have occurred. The stigma of slavery and the fear of Moslem contamination were also present. On the other hand, the slaves ought to marry female slaves, because, as a royal decree of 1527 put it, "with marriage and their love for wives and children and orderly married life they will become more calm and much sin and trouble will be avoided." In 1541, another decree along the same lines recommended marriage among Negroes, because of reports that had been received that the Negro slaves kept "great numbers of Indian women, some of them voluntarily, others against their wishes." [10] Viceroy Martín Enríquez of New Spain asked Philip II to secure from the Pope a strict prohibition against Afro-Indian marriage, or at least a clear statement that the children of such unions would automatically become slaves. But the king did not accept this proposal.[11] A century later, the town council of Santo Domingo, complaining that some Spanish officers had married Negro women, proposed to the king that such officers be excluded from further promotion in their career. With certain reservations the king approved of this discriminatory proposal in 1687.[12]

In 1776, the Crown issued solemn regulations governing marriage in Spain, which are very characteristic of the efforts made everywhere during this era to prevent socially unequal marriage. For those under twenty-five who wanted to contract marriage, the parents' approval was made a formal requirement. When these regulations were extended to the overseas possessions in 1778, this requirement was not to be applied to "Mulattoes, Negroes, Coyotes and other Castas and simi-

[9] Konetzke (1946b), 219, quoting chronicler Santa Clara.
[10] CDFS, I, 81–82, 99–100, 185, 210. See also Aguirre Beltrán (1946), 256–257.
[11] Marshall (1939), 173; CInd, 297–304.
[12] Rosenblat (1954), II, 159. See also Aguirre Beltrán (1946), 253.

lar races." Only colored officers of the militia had to fulfill the requirement in the same way as the whites. The legislator probably was influenced by prejudice, and also by the idea that *castas*, mixed-bloods, being usually illegitimate, would not be able to locate their fathers.[13] When the *audiencia* (high court and administrative council) of Chile received the marriage regulations, it replied that as far as Indians were concerned, "as their origin is not vile like that of other Castas . . . it would be unfair and irrational for Spanish parents, be it Europeans or Criollos, to oppose marriage with Indians." The Council of the Indies agreed and Indians were in fact given the same standing as Spaniards in the marriage regulations.[14] The audiencia of Mexico, too, caused the regulations to be clarified and rectified. It observed that mestizos and castizos "deserved to be set apart from the other Castas as was already done in some respects both in law and public esteem." Also in this case the Council agreed and mestizos and castizos were subjected to the same requirements as Spaniards. On the other hand, the Mexican audiencia, referring to the bad habits of Negroes and mulattoes, recommended that "special orders be given to the parish priests so that, in case some Indian wants to contract marriage with a person belonging to those Castas, both he and his parents . . . will receive a warning and explanation of the serious harm . . . that such unions will cause to themselves, their families and villages, besides making the descendants incapable of obtaining municipal positions of honor in which only pure Indians are allowed to serve." [15] The Council of the Indies in 1806 advised the king to reconfirm the liberty of marriage between Indians, "pure mestizos," and Spaniards. On the other hand, a royal decree of 1805 declared that persons of "pure blood" had to ask permission of the viceroy or the audiencia in order to marry "elements of Negro and Mulatto origin." [16] We can thus see that discriminatory policy in this respect became even more outspoken toward the end of the colonial period.

[13] The *Sanción Pragmática* of March 23, 1776 in CDFS, III, 406–413, the *Cédula explicativa* of 1778, *ibid.*, 438–442.

[14] *CDFS*, III, 466.

[15] *CDFS*, III, 477. When interpreting the *Pragmática* of 1776, the Crown attorney of the Council of the Indies in 1791 commented that "the difference of color . . . is really one of the causes that make for different condition and status of families" (*ibid.*, 696). Archbishop Lorenzana of Mexico in 1769 exhorted the Indians to marry their daughters to Spaniards but not to "castas." Mörner (1965a), 34.

[16] *CDFS*, III, 794–796; Aguirre Beltrán (1946), 253.

The Crown, the Church, and
Interracial Concubinage

Naturally enough the Church and, consequently, also the Crown opposed interracial concubinage as it did concubinage itself. This was also true of the stabilized relationship that was called *barraganía*, very frequent in Spain during the Middle Ages and tolerated by the *Siete partidas*, though later condemned by the Catholic kings. At the request of the Crown, the authorities sometimes took severe steps against those living in concubinage, who were thrown out of or fled from their places of residence. But little could in fact be done about it. "Those living in sin do not care about excommunication," a desperate prelate wrote in 1547.[17] Two hundred years later, traveler Antonio de Ulloa reports from the viceroyalty of Peru that concubinage was so frequent as to be considered completely normal. According to him, friars and priests also generally held concubines without even trying to hide it.[18] Because of the social structure in the Indies, the concubines of the whites were usually of darker skin. The Crown at times realized that the Indian partners in such relationships should not be judged too harshly. As early as 1505, the authorities were instructed that in lawsuits involving sexual offenses the Indian women should be treated with leniency, but the guilty Spaniards severely.[19] For all the efforts of state and Church, concubinage continued to provide the normal form for interethnic sexual relations. This fact, in turn, helps to explain the attitude of state and Church toward the people of mixed origin, who were automatically considered illegitimate.

The local authorities fought Afro-Indian concubinage with real ferocity. Several municipal ordinances of the sixteenth century imposed castration on the Negro as punishment, despite a royal decree that had already prohibited this savage penalty.[20] Afro-Indian concubinage, enforced by social conditions, continued nonetheless.

As elsewhere, the struggle of Crown and Church against concubinage was not considered incompatible with tolerating organized prosti-

[17] Borah and Cook (1966), 949–952; Konetzke (1946b), 223.

[18] Juan and Ulloa (1953), 374ff.

[19] Gutiérrez de Pineda (1963), 267.

[20] See, e.g., Rumazo González (1934), 386–388. This contradicts the view of Vial Correa (1947), 131–132, that the penalty was applied only in cases of rape.

40

tution, which appears early in the New World.[21] But we have Ulloa's word for it that in eighteenth-century Peru prostitution of the European type was lacking, a natural result of the high incidence of promiscuity in general.[22]

Ethnic Groups and Legal Status

Let us now briefly consider the legal status of each of the ethnic groups that composed colonial society. As I will show in Chapter V, a clear distinction must be made between legal condition and social status, even though there was an interplay between legislation and social reality. At least, prejudice and social conditions gradually influenced the Crown's policy and legislation.

The original pattern was very simple. There were two categories: "Spaniards" and "Indians." The former included Peninsular Spaniards, criollos, and legitimate mestizos. The Indians were to be free vassals and subjects of the Crown, and their caciques were granted the rank of hidalgos.[23] But theoretically the mass of the Indians were put on equal footing with the inferior stratum of Spanish society, that of "miserable rustics." From experience of Indian weaknesses and fear of Indian uprisings a peculiar collection of norms gradually took shape, defining the Indian's legal status. Liberties and obligations were neatly balanced. The Indians were to be governed by authorities of their own and ruled, partly, in accordance with their ancient customs, but they were specially supervised and their liberty of movement was restricted. They had to pay tribute to the king or to the encomendero and they also had to perform forced labor (*mita, cuatequil*). On the other hand, they were exempted from tithes (*diezmos*) and sales tax (*alcabala*). They were also exempted from military service but were not allowed to use firearms or swords or to ride on horseback. As "minors" they enjoyed special legal protection and were exempted from the jurisdiction of the Inquisition. On the same grounds they were not capable of concluding legal contracts, nor were they allowed to purchase wine.[24]

Negro slaves formed the third group that claimed special status.

[21] Ots Capdequí (1957), 121–122. Cf. Gutiérrez de Pineda (1963), 266.
[22] Juan and Ulloa (1953), 384–385.
[23] The nobility of Inca families was abolished in 1782 after the rebellion of Tupac was suppressed. *CDFS*, III, 482–483.
[24] A good summary in *Métodos* (1954), 62ff.

41

Since we take up the issue of slavery in a later chapter, it may suffice to mention here that the continuation of slavery in the Mediterranean since antiquity had assured the slaves certain elementary rights. But a comprehensive slave code for Spanish America was not issued until 1789.[25] Its relatively benign character distinguished it from earlier regulations of slavery, characterized mostly by their severity. Under Spanish law, however, manumission always existed as a possibility for slaves, though generally it depended on the will of the owner. As the slave condition of the mother dictated the bondage of the offspring, mulatto children also became slaves as a matter of course. But there were at least two kinds of legal escape for them: a royal decree, addressed to the officials of the exchequer in Cuba in 1583, considering that some Spanish soldiers there had sired children with slave women owned by the state and now wanted to purchase their freedom, ordered that the fathers be given preference at the auction where their children were to be sold.[26] The other exception dealt with the children of ecclesiastics with slave women. At least the first Mexican Council decreed that "if it so happens that an ecclesiastic . . . has had or maintains a lustful relationship with his slave . . . he should be punished according to law, and the Bishop dispose of the slave woman as he sees fit, and the children, if there are any, be set free. . . ."[27]

And what about the other elements of the population? Obviously, the increasingly numerous racially mixed and illegitimate people had not been anticipated by the early legislators. The disgust and desperation of the local authorities when faced with this phenomenon were shared by the Crown. A royal decree addressed to the viceroy of Peru in 1609 asked him to inform how "these people can be drawn off and the harm caused by their increase and bad ways diminished."[28] The attitude of the lawgiver seems to have been especially affected by the illegitimacy of the mixed-bloods.[29] The first legal restriction of their

[25] *CDFS*, III, 643–654.
[26] *CDFS*, I, 547.
[27] Aguirre Beltrán (1946), 263. Cf. 266–268.
[28] *CDFS*, II, 148.
[29] Referring mainly to royal bastards, Rosenblat (1954), II, 13–14, argues that natural sons were not disdained in Spain and Portugal. "If Spanish society lacked prejudice in this regard, American society was even less likely to be prejudiced. . . ." But Konetzke [IPGH (1961), 61] rejects this argument by referring to the inferiority attributed to illegitimates in Spanish law and to the objections of the Council of the Indies against large-scale legitimization of "natural sons."

rights was introduced in 1549, when it was decreed that "no Mulatto, nor Mestizo or person who is born out of wedlock be allowed to have Indians [in encomienda]." [30] The words "mestizo" and "illegitimate" had become almost synonymous. The fact of their illegitimacy made the mixed-bloods unfit to supervise and to be in close contact with the Indians. Grievances over their bad conduct continually reached the Council of the Indies. To this were added the fears (on the whole, groundless) that the mestizos would not be loyal in an Indian rebellion or an attack of pirates. In the 1570's, a series of legal restrictions on the capacity of the mestizos was enacted. They were excluded from the positions of Protector of Indians, Notary Public, as well as cacique, and were also prohibited from living among the Indians. In 1643, they were also deprived of the right of becoming soldiers.[31] Juan de Solórzano Pereira, the great expert on Spanish American law of the time, interpreted these restrictions as applying only to illegitimates and was generally displeased with their exclusion from the career of arms. Comparing them with mulattoes and *zamboes* (Afro-Indian mixed bloods), Solórzano, who had spent many years in Peru, exclaimed that the "Mestizos are the best mixture that exists in the Indies." [32]

The controversy over ordaining mestizos as priests is particularly interesting because the pride and exclusivism of the Church, as a corporation, was directly involved. At the same time, priests who knew the native languages were in great demand; and such priests might most easily be recruited among the mestizos. In 1568, Philip II prohibited mestizos from being ordained "for many reasons," but some years later the pope permitted the ordination of "illegitimates and Mestizos" if they were personally virtuous and familiar with native languages. In 1588, Philip II also chose to accept ordination of mestizos if it were preceded by a thorough investigation of the antecedents

[30] *CDFS*, I, 256. Cf. II, 32 and Ots Capdequí (1957), 125–126.

[31] Konetzke (1960), 113–129.

[32] Solórzano Pereira (1647), book II, ch. XXX, §§ 35, 38. He also makes a strict distinction between legitimate and illegitimate mestizos and mulattoes, concluding that "generally they are born in adultery and in other illicit and ugly unions, because there are few Spaniards of honor who marry Indians or Negroes. This defect of their birth makes them infamous [to which are added] the stain of different color and other vices that are natural for them and suckled with the milk" (§ 20). When receiving a royal decree of 1653 forbidding mestizos, mulattoes, and Negroes to carry swords, Viceroy Salvatierra of Peru did not apply it to the mestizos, who were "the most capable ones, property owners and friends of the Spaniards. . . ." Polo (1899), II, 47.

of the candidates, who had to be legitimate. These conditions often served the prelates as a welcome pretext for practically excluding the mestizos from priesthood. In convents, a similar exclusivism was displayed.[33]

During the eighteenth century the frequency of legitimate mestizos probably increased considerably; we have already seen that the marriage regulations of 1778 were modified in their favor. Indian ancestry was not to be considered "vile." In 1790, the King explicitly declared that "information on the purity of blood should not include the Indian race among bad and deficient races." [34]

On the other hand, mulattoes, zamboes, and free Negroes all suffered from the combination of illegitimacy and the stigma of slavery. In addition to the restrictions imposed on the mestizos, they were liable to pay tribute like the Indians.[35] They might be sent to forced labor in the mines, but should then work apart from the Indians to prevent them from abusing the natives. Their movements were restricted, their dress was regulated, and they were strictly prohibited from owning firearms.[36] Nevertheless, people of African blood were able to demonstrate their military value in emergencies, and, little by little, they were recruited to form special militia units. In this military context, mulattoes were called *pardos* and Negroes *morenos*. The members of these militia units were exempted from tribute and, as the eighteenth century proceeded, they also came to enjoy, at least partly, the privilege of being placed under military jurisdiction, the *fuero militar*.[37] People of African blood were finally excluded by law from receiving doctorates. In 1768, this was justified by reference to "a great

---

[33] Konetzke (1946b), 231–232; Chamberlin (1966), who stresses regional differences. During the later colonial period the lack of priests weakened exclusivism. The archbishop of Santo Domingo in 1706 even asked the king for permission to ordain mulattoes, while restricting their possibilities of promotion. This was approved. *CDFS*, III, 107–108. Cf. 821–829.

[34] *CDFS*, III, 687.

[35] Bishop Manuel Abad y Quipo comments: "The Castas are infamous by law, being descended from Negro slaves. They are liable to tribute . . . and tribute is for them an indelible mark of slavery that they are unable to erase with the passing of time or by mixing with other races in successive generations. There are many of them who by their color, features and behavior would rise to the class of "Spaniards" but for this impediment that leaves them depressed in the same class." Mora (1963), 205.

[36] *CDFS*, I, 213, 482–483; II, 47, 182, 184, etc.

[37] McAlister (1957), ch. IV; Rosenblat (1954), II, 157–158; *CDFS*, II, 334; III, 325.

many lawyers of obscure birth and bad ways." [38] The "most vile birth" of zamboes and mulattoes was considered a fact beyond discussion.

The latter half of the eighteenth century, as we shall see, witnessed the culmination of socioracial prejudice against the mulattoes or pardos. Though the leaders of government obviously were imbued with the same prejudice as others, they nevertheless launched a new policy, permitting wealthy pardos to purchase licenses, so-called *cédulas de gracias al sacar*, that made them legally white. This policy became increasingly generous. In 1783, the application of a very distinguished pardo, Bernardo Ramírez, who wanted to improve his legal quality, was categorically rejected. But, to take another concrete example, in 1796, a certain Julián Valenzuela, on the basis of his "ways, education and habits," seems to have obtained his license easily.[39] This policy must have been dictated by financial considerations (a tariff was issued in 1801) as well as by a desire to counterbalance politically an increasingly suspect criollo elite. A student of the matter, James King, concludes that the intention was "to compensate individual merits among the subjects of color, to drain the possible leader force from the colored masses by creating, at the same time, partisans grateful to the Crown who added to the white minority and undermined the pretensions of the criollo aristocracy." [40] In any case, the cedulas de gracias al sacar reveal the extent of the ambitions of absolute monarchy. A document of 1783 states that the king "in virtue of his sovereignty is able to draw any vassal whatever from the obscurity of his birth to place him in a distinguished sphere." [41]

The Racial Separation Policy

The Crown pursued rather tenaciously a policy intended to separate its Indian subjects from the others.[42] The point of departure of this policy was the concept of the two republics, the *República de españoles* and the *República de indios*. In the early days this dualism was natural, but it was soon undermined by race mixture. Whereas the early mis-

[38] *CDFS*, III, 340. On the other hand, after 1797 they were allowed to become physicians. Depons (1960), I, 124–125.
[39] *CDFS*, III, 530–535, 754.
[40] King (1951), 644. The *Gracias al Sacar* bear great similarity to the system of "assimilados" in twentieth-century Portuguese Africa.
[41] *CDFS*, III, 434.
[42] This topic, until then largely unexplored, is studied by Mörner (1961a, 1964b, 1966a, 1966b), Mörner and Gibson (1962).

sionaries arriving in the Indies had expected the Spaniards to set a good example for the Indians, later on both ecclesiastics and many administrators, taught by bitter experience, became convinced that Spaniards and mestizos were really more of a bad example to the neophytes. As exemplified by the mission of the famous Dominican, Bartolomé de Las Casas, in the "Land of True Peace" in Guatemala, missionaries preferred to work without intervention by other whites. Spanish and mestizo vagrants very soon infested Indian villages. This social problem motivated the prohibitions against vagrants living among the Indians, enacted in 1536 and 1563. Abuses were also committed by the encomenderos and their overseers (calpisques), often Negro slaves or freedmen whom the encomenderos left in the villages of their Indians. Consequently, Negro calpisques were forbidden to reside among the Indians in 1541, calpisques in general in 1550 (modified later on), and, finally, the encomenderos themselves in 1563.[43] The systematic exclusion of all mestizos, mulattoes, and Negroes followed in 1578, at the suggestion of an Augustinian friar from Peru.[44] Pure Spaniards finally were added to the list in 1600. Even non-Indians who owned land within an Indian village were forbidden to settle there, it was explained in 1646.[45] On the other hand, mestizos who had been brought up by their Indian mothers in a village were excepted. The laws enforcing residential separation were included in the *Recopilación* of 1680.[46] The background of this policy, formed principally during the 1570's, was the rapid decline of the Indian population, the systematic gathering of the remaining Indians into large mission villages, *reducciones* or *congregaciones*, and the increasing disorders in the countryside attributed to vagrants and mixed-bloods. The motivations of the policy were several. In the first place, the Crown wanted to protect the Indians not only from violence and abuse but also from influences harmful to their morals and faith. Second, there was a desire to maintain the dualism already established in the ecclesiastical and administrative realms. "Spaniards" could not be subjected to the jurisdiction of "Indian" town councils, nor should the cure of their souls be entrusted to friars or priests whose function was that of missionaries. Consequently, "Spaniards" and "Indians" ought to live

[43] Mörner (1964a).
[44] Mörner (1962).
[45] The background of this *Cédula* is in Mörner (1965b).
[46] *RI*, book VI, title III, 21–23, etc.

apart, in villages or towns of their own. In fact, the policy of separation may also have been aimed at promoting the founding of new "Spanish" centers.[47] This policy was not discriminatory in the same way as South African "apartheid," or, at least, the discrimination was not directed against the Indians but rather against the non-Indians. Segregation imposed to lessen interethnic tension and to provide autonomy becomes discrimination only if compulsorily imposed on one or several groups (as it usually is). In Spanish America, the Indians applauded the policy of separation or segregation. Thus the victims of segregation in this case were rather the mestizos, mulattoes, and other non-Indians.

The policy of separation, though less emphasized than in the rural environment, was also imposed in the cities, where the Indians were supposed to live in special districts, such as the famous Cercado of Lima. When set to work in mines or textile workshops (*obrajes de paño*) the Indians, according to the law, would have to be kept apart from other workers.

Theoretically, the policy of separation implied a conflict with another aim of the Crown: spreading Spanish among the Indians, which was proclaimed with emphasis in a royal decree of 1770.[48] Nor did this policy harmonize with the liberty of Spanish-Indian intermarriage, even if, as we have just noticed, intermarriage was never promoted by the Crown. On the other hand, the aversion of the Crown and the authorities to Afro-Indian miscegenation was, of course, in keeping with the policy of separation. That is why a 1781 document on intermarriage refers explicitly to "the laws that prohibit contact and communication between Indians and Mulattoes, Negroes and similar races." [49]

The conflict between the different aims of the Crown that could be envisioned, especially during the eighteenth century, never really materialized because at that time the policy of separation had failed completely. This had been true as early as 1680 when the very laws of separation were codified. The Crown simply lacked the tools with which to impose such a radical policy, especially when it was not systematically supplemented by new towns, founded to harbor "Spaniards," Negroes, and castas. Because of the decline of the Indian

[47] The additional motives for separating Negroes from Indians are discussed by Mörner (1966b).

[48] Mörner (1967).

[49] *CDFS*, III, 477. It was not a new prohibition, as erroneously claimed by Rosenblat (1954), II, 147, and others.

47

population and the increase of the mestizos, the policy proved increasingly absurd. Although theoretically in force, the laws of separation were applied only in isolated cases from about 1680 onward, giving rise to interminable lawsuits. It was only in the missions situated in peripheral regions, such as those of the Jesuits among the Guaraníes in Río de la Plata, that the laws still were applied, because they suited the missionaries.[50] During his famous tour of inspection in New Spain, *Visitador* José Galvez declared in 1767 that in the future the laws of separation should be applied only in mission districts. But theoretically the obsolete laws were abolished only as a result of emancipation.

In trying to summarize the politico-legal aspect of race relations in Spanish America during the colonial period, I find it impossible to speak about a tolerant and generous attitude. But it would be anachronistic and unfair to characterize this attitude as "racist." The attitude of the Spanish Crown simply has to be evaluated in the context of the hierarchic concept of society that held sway in the Western world prior to the French revolution. In Spanish America, this same concept was being applied in a multiracial, colonial environment. Advising the king, the Council of the Indies expresses this very eloquently in 1806: ". . . if it is impossible to deny that the different hierarchies and strata are of the greatest value to the monarchical state because their gradual and connected links of subordination and dependence support and substantiate the obedience and respect of the lowest vassal towards the King, this system is required for many more reasons in America. This is so, not only because of the greater distance from the Throne but because of the great number of people who by their vicious origin and nature cannot be compared with simple people in Spain and do constitute a very inferior species. It would be utterly reprehensible if those known to be sons and descendants of slaves sat down with those who derive from the first conquistadores or families that are noble, legitimate, white and free from any ugly stain." [51]

As we shall see more clearly in Chapter V, the Crown, in its "racial" policy, usually reflected rather than influenced prevalent attitudes. But it is also true that at times it tried, though with little success, to modify extreme social attitudes for one reason or another.[52]

[50] Mörner (1961b).

[51] *CDFS*, III, 825.

[52] Other students of the matter give more importance to the role of the Crown in forming and maintaining the social system. See Konetzke (1951); Beneyto (1961), 232; McAlister (1963), 365.

Portugal's Racial Policy in Brazil

The basic conditions and motivations of the "racial" policy of Portugal in America were very similar to those of Spain. But in this as in other fields, Portuguese colonial administration was looser and weaker. Thus the gulf between legislation and social reality became even wider. Perhaps this is why Portuguese legislation in Brazil has been studied relatively little.

The Church and Crown probably tolerated Portuguese-Indian intermarriage from the beginning, but such marriages seem to have been very few. In 1551, Jesuit Superior Nóbrega reported from Pernambuco that the settlers found it "a great infamy" to marry Indian women.[53] He repeatedly urged the king to send orphan girls and even women of bad reputation from Portugal to Brazil at the request of the settlers, who preferred to marry whites. This attitude obviously was shared by the Crown. When it is asserted in a well-known book that "Portuguese policy was consistently *in favor* of mixed marriage *until* the eighteenth century," [54] the author fails to give evidence for this statement. We do know that in the middle of the eighteenth century a remarkable statesman, the Marquess of Pombal, suddenly introduced a policy in favor of Portuguese-Indian intermarriage. The principal passage of the famous *Alvará de lei* of April 4, 1755, runs as follows:

> . . . those of my vassals of this kingdom [Portugal] and America who marry Indians will remain without infamy by this act. They will, on the contrary, be worthy of my royal attention and where they settle down they will be preferred for the positions that correspond to their rank. Their sons and descendants will be worthy and capable of receiving any kind of position, honor and dignity without need to be granted any exception. . . .[55]

There is an antecedent to this surprising decree in the instructions sent by Pombal in 1751 to Governor Gomes Freire de Andrade, then in charge of demarcating the border with the Spanish territories of Río de la Plata. The great problems of this demarcation were the populous Guaraní Missions of Spanish Jesuits along the existing border. Pombal therefore admonished the governor to attract the Guaraní In-

[53] Nóbrega (1955), 91.
[54] *Ibid.*, 29–30, 79–80, 102, 114. Such prostitutes might be sent who had not "entirely lost their sense of shame. . . ."
[55] Andrade (1961), document I.

dians to settle on the Portuguese side of the border in order to populate these desolate areas. The best means of attracting them, he wrote, would be to follow the example of the Romans and of Affonso d'Albuquerque in East India. He was referring to the Portuguese policy in India from 1510 onward, which promoted intermarriage with women of the higher castes, for clearly political reasons.[56] This, Pombal went on, required the use of two methods. In the first place, all legal differences between Portuguese and Guaraní Indians must be abolished and special distinctions must be awarded to Portuguese who intermarry. The offspring of intermarriages should enjoy the same privileges as the Portuguese. Second, Indian administration should be the best possible. Furthermore, it should be strictly forbidden to ridicule the Indians by calling them barbarians and their sons "Mestiços and other epithets of derision and insult." [57] Against this background, Pombal's sensational policy with regard to mixed marriages seems to have grown out of two main considerations. First, it was an element in his mercantilist policy of promoting population growth, thereby strengthening the border. Second, it was a way of attracting the Indians, who until then had been under the tutelage of the Spanish Jesuits in Río de la Plata and of their Portuguese brethren in the Amazon. Thus it fitted in with his relentless struggle against the Society of Jesus. It is more difficult to say whether or not Pombal's policy should also in part be attributed to the influence of the idea of "le bon sauvage." [58]

Pombal's "liberal" policy regarding mixed marriage did not extend to the African element. In 1771, the viceroy of Brazil lowered the rank of an Indian (!) military officer for having proved to be "so low minded a person as to marry a Negro woman, blemishing his blood by this alliance." [59] If the marriage between Indian and Negro was considered to be contrary to "purity of blood," it is easy to imagine what would have been the reaction if a white officer had married a Negro. There is no reason to believe that Pombal's and the metropolitan government's

[56] Boxer (1963), 64–65, 76–77.

[57] Carneiro de Mendonça (1960), 188–189.

[58] Cf. Boxer (1963), 98; Teixeira Soares (1961), 186. On the efforts of the Governor of Pará-Maranhão, Francisco Xavier de Mendonça Furtado, to enforce the decree of 1755, see Carneiro de Mendonça (1963), II, 759; III, 948, 977. In the words of the governor: ". . . this is the real way . . . of populating this enormously vast country."

[59] Buarque de Holanda (1956), 58. Cf. the decree of 1726 making the municipal posts a monopoly of whites married to whites. *Ibid.*, 28–29; Boxer (1963), 116–117.

view of intermarriage with Negro partners was any more "enlightened" than that of this viceroy.

In his widely read work, Angel Rosenblat affirms that the Portuguese policy "favored race mixture even without religious consecration" in order to populate Brazil.[60] But he gives no evidence of such an extraordinary attitude on the part of the Crown. Lack of action against concubinage by lax administrators and immoral ecclesiastics cannot be interpreted as a policy. In fact, the Crown and the authorities combatted especially pernicious forms of the promiscuity prevalent in Brazil, such as hiring out slave women as prostitutes. But it was an unsuccessful struggle.[61]

Under the Portuguese system the legal standing of the different ethnic groups coincided by and large with that under the Spanish. The Crown did make some efforts (in 1688, 1698, and 1714) to prohibit very severe corporal punishment of Negro slaves, but otherwise the institution of slavery was given little attention by the Crown and the authorities. The abolition of slavery in Portugal itself, decreed by Pombal in 1761, did not affect Brazil.[62] Even Indian slavery proved very difficult to abolish there. According to a law of 1570, Indians captured in a "just war" might be enslaved, but later the terms were made more generous for the slavers. In 1605 and 1609, Indian slavery was categorically forbidden, but soon modifications were again introduced. The concession that Indians already kept in slavery by other Indians (*indios de corda*, because they were supposed to be tied with a cord) might be enslaved proved a very convenient excuse for slave hunters. In the Amazon and in the Maranhão a long and dramatic struggle raged between the white settlers and the Jesuits over Indian freedom or bondage. It ended in a kind of compromise. The Indians for the fields of the former and for the missions of the latter were procured by both violence and peaceful persuasion.[63] It was only during the secularization of the Jesuit missions in 1755–1758 that Pombal

[60] Rosenblat (1954), II, 100–101. His affirmation that "Portuguese laws . . . fathered (*prohijaban*) natural sons" would also deserve to be scrutinized; Cf. Borah and Cook (1966), 949–952.

[61] Boxer (1962), 165. It is true, however, that Nóbrega accused other ecclesiastics for conceding absolution very generously in cases of concubinage. Nóbrega (1955), 102 and *passim*.

[62] Boxer (1962), 9; (1963), 100, 103. The law was probably mainly due to the protests of free laborers against slave competition. Verlinden (1955), 839.

[63] Boxer (1962), 279–280.

solemnly declared the Indian legally emancipated, an emancipation on paper that very soon proved completely illusory.

Portuguese legislation, like social attitudes, clearly distinguished between mestiços and other mixed-bloods. Free Negroes and mulattoes were forbidden to carry arms and to wear expensive clothes. Crimes committed by them were to be punished more severely. But despite the obstacles, some pardos knew how to obtain education and wealth. Even among the Negroes the customary discrimination was subject to exceptions. Thus the Negro Henrique Dias, hero of the mid-seventeenth century struggle against the Dutch in the northeast, was accepted into the Order of Christ. In 1759, distinguished mulattoes were given the privilege of carrying swords.[64]

The Spanish Crown's efforts to accomplish residential separation between the Indians and others had no counterpart in Brazil. Even the Jesuit missionaries were too closely related to the surrounding whites and mixed-bloods to request royal confirmation of such a policy.

An exhaustive and objective study of the socioracial policy of the Crown in Brazil remains to be done. Thanks to the revisionist approach of the British historian C. R. Boxer, the traditional concept of a consistently tolerant Portuguese policy in racial matters has finally been challenged. But more systematic investigations will be needed to ascertain to what extent Boxer's view deserves to be accepted.

[64] Boxer (1962), 166; (1963), 106, 116–117.

V

The Society of Castes: Rise and Decline

The Spanish American Society of Castes

Society in Spanish America during the Conquest was relatively open, as we have seen, but the period of colonization witnessed a society gradually becoming more and more closed and rigidly stratified. This society is known as the Society of Castes (*Sociedad* or *Régimen de Castas*), but it differed strikingly from the East Indian prototype. Society in Spanish America was not divided into strictly endogamous groups; some vertical social mobility existed and the system enjoyed no explicit religious sanction.

In fact, we may reasonably suspect that the contemporary use of the word "casta" for the mixed, popular strata has unduly influenced analyses by later students. But "casta" is a medieval, Iberian word that might designate any kind of animal or human group. When the Portuguese became acquainted with the peculiar social system of Hindu India, they used the word to describe it and the name stuck. The semantics did not, of course, remain the same when the word was used in the New World.[1] Consequently, the Sociedad de Castas of Spanish America did not necessarily correspond to the caste type of social

[1] Corominas (1954), 722–724. In the community of Vicos, Ancash, Peru, the word "casta" is being used about consanguineous kin groups. Vázquez (1964).

stratification. The division of society into groups invested with different legal status as well as the strong element of corporative privileges suggest that it is, in fact, closer to another system of stratification, that of estates. Also, the limited vertical social mobility of the time is consistent with this pattern. On the other hand, the feudal European correlation between sociolegal status and relationship to the land did not apply, nor were any representative political functions delegated to the different strata as in Europe during the late Middle Ages.[2] It is true that during the colonial period, an emerging system of economic classes can be discerned, in the rural sector rather than in the urban. But, as I hope to be able to show, it was the Régimen de Castas that continued to supply the social values, and it was sanctioned in law until the end of the period. There is no reason to believe that, as Marxist interpreters argue, it was only a thin veil cast over a reality of economic classes and class conflict. Such an approach does in fact seem to be insufficient and even anachronistic for analyzing any Western society prior to the French revolution.[3] In addition, Spanish America obviously was retarded in its social evolution. As we see it, the Spanish American Society of Castes certainly was a society *sui generis*, but it was created by transferring to the New World the hierarchic, estate-based, corporative society of late medieval Castile and imposing that society upon a multiracial, colonial situation. This colonial reality was characterized, first, by the dichotomy between conquerors and conquered, masters and servants or slaves, and, second, by the miscegenation between these opposite groups. Hence it was inevitable that social stratification and social status would become closely related to the division into ethnic groups. The location of the existing ethnic groups within the hierarchic social structure gave rise to what a Chilean student has ingeniously called "pigmentocracy." [4] People were classified in accordance with the color of their skin, with the white masters occupying the highest stratum. Theoretically, each group that could be racially defined would constitute a social stratum of its own.

But the complex pigmentocratic system emerged slowly and gradually. In the beginning, as we have already mentioned, dualism prevailed with "Christians" or "Spaniards" on the one side, and Indians

[2] Góngora (1951), 178–183; R. Morse in Hartz (1964), 144; McAlister (1963).

[3] As does, e.g., Bagú (1952), 102. Cf. McAlister (1963), 362.

[4] Lipschütz (1944), 75 and *passim*, and other works by the same author.

on the other. The first mestizos were being absorbed by one or the other parental group. In 1533, Emperor Charles ordered the audiencia of Mexico to gather all "the sons of Spaniards born of Indian women . . . and living with the Indians" and to give them Spanish education and training.[5] And not a few of the first mestizos deserved to be accepted by society, despite their illegitimate birth, because they had been recognized by their fathers. But the increase in illegitimate mestizos, left to the care of their Indian mothers, inevitably produced a special group that was not accepted by either parental group. On the other hand, mestizos born in wedlock, at least during the sixteenth century, were accepted as criollos; that is, "American Spaniards." [6] It was natural, then, that the word "mestizo" became almost synonymous with "illegitimate." The disdain and the prejudice of those occupying the highest stratum was therefore easily nurtured by the illegitimacy of the lower strata. This disdain imbued and helped to keep the hierarchic social system together. For the African element, slavery provided an additional stigma and cause of disdain. The medieval concepts of religious orthodoxy in the Iberian Peninsula, "purity of the blood" and "pride of lineage," were transferred to the New World as a matter of course.[7] Only "old Christians," unsuspected of any religious contamination, be it Jewish or Moorish, were in fact permitted to migrate to Spanish America. This legal restriction made it easy for the Spaniards arriving in America to adopt a social attitude, and enabled them to pursue ambitions that in Europe were monopolized by the aristocracy. At the same time, they identified the dark-skinned members of the lower strata with the "vile" plebeians of the traditional European society. Nobody has analyzed this process better than Alexander von Humboldt, the intelligent observer of Spanish America during the first years of the nineteenth century. "In Spain it is a kind of title of nobility not to descend from Jews or Moors. In America, the skin, more or less white, is what dictates the class that an individual occupies in society. A white, even if he rides barefoot on horseback, considers himself a

[5] CDFS, I, 147. See also 168.

[6] Aguirre Beltrán (1946), 250, believes that the distinction between legitimate sons of Indo-Spanish unions who were called Spaniards or criollos, and illegitimate ones who were called mestizos, had been established by 1570.

[7] The distinction made by Beltrán (1946), 271, between "old Christians" and those "pure in blood" is hardly justified, since both concepts were based on a religious criterion.

member of the nobility of the country." [8] Another factor of interest here has been pointed out by a Spanish historian, studying the antagonism between peninsular Spaniards and criollos. The former inculpated the latter "their drops of Mestizo blood, and consequently both exaggerated their racial pride in being whites with corresponding disdain for the people of color." [9]

Prejudice and Socioracial Terminology

One often meets with the argument that prejudice in Spanish American colonial society was social and not racial, since it came about because whites occupied the upper stratum.[10] It may be true that the prejudice in question did not as a rule express itself in feelings or actions of repugnance for certain defined phenotypes. But it is certainly hazardous if not impossible to distinguish clearly between racial prejudice and social prejudice: the latter very often precedes the former. Even if one does not accept the Marxist position that prejudice is *only* an invention with which to defend economic self-interest, the whole controversy seems utterly devoid of interest. What matters is the relationship that existed in Spanish America between social (and even legal) status and the color of the skin.[11]

A contemporary, Bartolomé de Góngora, tells a rather amusing story in his book *El Corregidor Sagaz* (1656) that illustrates well prevailing attitudes and prejudices:

One day, Don Juan Pareja, well known in Mexico for his great quality, canon of the Holy Church there and illustrious for his sayings and actions, was touring the streets of the city. Then he met an old, well dressed and white haired Mulatto. Having brought the coach to a stop he asked the Pardo to approach and asked him: "What is your name?" The Pardo told him, whereupon the canon exclaimed: "In

[8] Humboldt (1941), II, 262. The viceroy of Peru complained in 1806 that many "lazy vagabonds" arrived from Spain, being attracted by "the greater consideration that they enjoy in these parts without any discrimination, owing to the single quality of white skin." Romero (1901), 37. On the socioracial pride that imbued "caste society," Juan and Ulloa (1768), I, 32, report: "Every person is so jealous of the order of their tribe or Cast, that if through inadvertence, without the least intention to affront, you call them by a degree lower than what they actually are, they are highly offended. . . ."
[9] G. Céspedes in Vicens Vives, III (1957), 503.
[10] Even stated by Konetzke (1946b), 229.
[11] The Marxist position is intelligently represented by Bagú (1952), 54. On prejudice in general, see Allport (1958).

all my readings I have never come across a Mulatto Saint and Mulattoes cannot become Saints. God bless you, I am going to canonize you because a Mulatto who seems to be honorable and who has grown as much white hair without being hanged or stabbed to death, must be a Saint." [12]

In the eighteenth century, socioracial prejudice in Spanish America, by analogy with what happened elsewhere at the time, was obviously on the increase. Even so keen and intelligent an observer as the young Spanish officer Antonio de Ulloa, together with his companion Jorge Juan, after their visit to the Peruvian viceroyalty in the 1730's, proposed that the mestizos, vicious and of no use in their native land as they were, should be deported to Spain to recruit some regiments submitted to rigorous discipline. But they still should be kept apart from the whites so as not to become arrogant because of their familiarity with them.[13] The disdain of both Spaniards and criollos for mestizos and other "castas" was as good as boundless. Only a few exceptional figures like Dean Antonio García Redondo of Guatemala and Bishop Manuel Abad y Quipo of Michoacán, Mexico, were able to realize that if "castas" behaved badly, their acts could be explained by the legal discrimination and poverty that they were suffering.[14]

Socioracial terminology, more precisely elaborated in the eighteenth century, always reflected disdain.[15] Already Inca Garcilaso de la Vega affirms that ". . . if in the Indies . . . one is told 'you are a Mestizo' it is regarded as an expression of contempt." The Inca states that this name, "imposed by our fathers" and referring to the mixture of two great nations, only made him proud.[16] The opposite reaction undoubtedly was much more frequent. A contemporary observer in Paraguay remarks that the inhabitants were quite distinguished ". . . so that it

[12] B. Góngora (1960), 235. Though the author admits that there are some good mestizos, mulattoes, and Negroes, he declares that "most are ungrateful and thankless," a great fault in a hierarchic society.

[13] Juan and Ulloa (1953), 133–134. A similar proposal was made by an Augustinian friar in 1575. Lissón Chávez, no. 10, 798. Viceroy Revillagigedo (Jr.) in 1794 lamented the lack of European immigrants in New Spain "who might have improved in many ways the Indian race." He also states that Negroes "have disfigured and deteriorated the Indian caste in many ways and have given rise to all the ugly castes that can be seen in these kingdoms. . . ." *Instruciones*, II (1873), 52.

[14] Mörner (1965), 39–42.

[15] Aguirre Beltrán (1946), 72.

[16] Vega (1959), 566–567. "Mestizo" is derived from *mixticius* (popular Latin) and simply means "mixed." Corominas, III, 315–316.

was not fitting to call them Mestizos but rather *Montañeses*, the term that they appreciated." [17] The nomenclatures of "castas" were developing with the times. They also show remarkable regional differences and variations.[18] As an example, we present the following list from eighteenth-century New Spain:

1. Spaniard and Indian beget mestizo
2. Mestizo and Spanish woman beget castizo
3. Castizo woman and Spaniard beget Spaniard [19]
4. Spanish woman and Negro beget mulatto [20]
5. Spaniard and mulatto woman beget morisco [21]
6. Morisco woman and Spaniard beget albino
7. Spaniard and albino woman beget torna atrás
8. Indian and torna atrás woman beget lobo
9. Lobo and Indian woman beget zambaigo
10. Zambaigo and Indian woman beget cambujo
11. Cambujo and mulatto woman beget albarazado
12. Albarazado and mulatto woman beget barcino
13. Barcino and mulatto woman beget coyote
14. Coyote woman and Indian beget chamiso
15. Chamiso woman and mestizo beget coyote mestizo
16. Coyote mestizo and mulatto woman beget ahí te estás

Another series of words illustrates the Peruvian nomenclature during the same period:

1. Spaniard and Indian woman beget mestizo
2. Spaniard and mestizo woman beget cuarterón de mestizo
3. Spaniard and cuarterona de mestizo beget quinterón
4. Spaniard and quinterona de mestizo beget Spaniard or requinterón de mestizo
5. Spaniard and Negress beget mulatto
6. Spaniard and mulatto woman beget quarterón de mulato
7. Spaniard and cuarterona de mulato beget quinterón
8. Spaniard and quinterona de mulato beget requinterón

[17] Cardozo (1959), 69.
[18] See, e.g., Rosenblat (1954), II, 173–179; Aguirre Beltrán (1946), 175–178; Varallanos (1962), 66–70.
[19] Comment by Rosenblat (1954), II, 137: "We are, hence, rather distant from an extreme racist conception in this society." Cf. the Peruvian nomenclature given in our text, nos. 4 and 9.
[20] Derived from *mulo* (Latin), comparing the hybrid origin of the mulatto with that of the mule. Corominas, III, 475.
[21] A royal decree in 1700 prohibited the use of this term to avoid confusion with the identical Spanish word for "converted Moor." CDFS, III, 81–82.

9. Spaniard and requinterona de mulato beget white people
10. Mestizo and Indian woman beget cholo
11. Mulatto and Indian woman beget chino [22]
12. Spaniard and china beget cuarterón de chino
13. Negro and Indian woman beget sambo de Indio
14. Negro and mulatto woman beget zambo

These examples do not by any means exhaust the terminology. Innumerable more or less strange names have been documented: *no te entiendo, tente en el aire, jíbaro, tresalbo, jarocho, sambo prieto, lunarejo, mequimixt, rayado,* etc.[23] Now it should be made quite clear that we cannot take all these terms seriously. We find them, above all, in the explanatory notes on a number of well-known eighteenth-century paintings illustrating racial crosses in Spanish America, nowadays preserved in museums in Mexico, Madrid, and Vienna. We also find them listed in the works of learned authors of the time. In other words, most of these terms are artificial, being the products of a few intellectuals and artists. Furthermore, they illustrate the almost pathological interest in genealogy that is characteristic of the age. The paintings often show a striking contrast, realistically representing each individual in his special dress but in the most unlikely combinations of subjects, absurd especially in those days, such as an elegantly dressed Spaniard with a typically clad Indian or Negro woman. This suggests that we have to do with an entertaining genre of art, characteristic rather of eighteenth-century exoticism and rococo than of a serious effort to present the social reality of the Indies.

The complexity and confusion of the erudite nomenclatures show convincingly that the genealogical criterion of ethnic classification had become completely absurd, especially in dealing with people who more often than not were illegitimate. On the other hand, only a few distinctions could be made on the basis of the phenotype or appearance alone. Perhaps, of all the terms mentioned above, besides the basic Spaniard, mestizo, mulatto, Indian, and zambo, the only ones frequently used were coyote and cholo, both indicating dark mestizo, and castizo or bright mestizo. The parish priests generally kept three separate registers, one for "Spaniards," another for *"castas de mezcla"*

[22] According to Humboldt, II (1941), 140–141, the offspring of Indian and Negro were called *chinos* in both Mexico and Peru, whereas *zambo* was a Venezuelan expression.

[23] Rosenblat (1954), II, 168–173; León (1924), 21–27; Blanchard (1908–1910).

(mixed castes), and a third one for "Indians." [24] In these registers people were classified, more or less, in the basic categories just mentioned.

Race and Social Stratification

How closely did the ethnic terms correspond to defined strata within the social structure? A recent student believes that there were in fact only three legally and socially definable groups: "Spaniards," "castas," and "Indians." [25] I think, however, that the distinction between mestizos on the one hand, and on the other free Negroes, mulattoes, and zamboes is far too important to be ignored. As the Bishop of Caracas affirmed in 1805: "in these provinces, the Mulattoes have never been reputed Mestizos or been confused with them. . . ." Although the mestizos were located close to the whites, the mulattoes were definitely people "fit for service, be it slave work or unskilled jobs." [26] I believe also that two scales of classification can be clearly distinguished within the Sociedad de Castas, one of them sanctioned in law, the other corresponding to social status. Though the whites enjoyed the superior position in both, the differences are obvious:

A. *Legal condition*
1. "Spaniards"
2. Indians
3. Mestizos
4. Free Negroes, mulattoes, zamboes
5. Slaves

B. *Social status*
1. Peninsular Spaniards
2. Criollos
3. Mestizos
4. Mulattoes, zamboes, free Negroes
5. Slaves
6. Indians (if not caciques, etc.)

Though legally superior to the mixed people, especially those of African descent, the Indian's social position was undoubtedly the most inferior. "Castas" knew Spanish and were the servants, slaves, or employees of the Spaniards. Therefore, in the words of José Miranda, they appeared "in the eyes of the natives as reflections of the authority of

[24] Konetzke (1946a). Tariffs for church services were differentiated on an ethnic basis, as shown by an example from Peru in 1583. Lissón Chávez, no. 13 (1945), 254–258. Whereas a Spanish funeral must not cost more than 14 pesos, that of an Indian married to a Spaniard or mestizo should cost 5, that of a Negro or a Yanacona Indian 2, and that of a Mita Indian 1 peso only.
[25] McAlister (1963), 356.
[26] Leal (1963), 329.

their masters." [27] Even contemporary observers became aware of the contradiction between legal and social status. Speaking about conditions in Rio de la Plata, Félix de Azara remarks that "the law places the Mulatto in the last place, after the Europeans and their sons, Indians, Mestizos and even Negroes, but public opinion ranks them as equals of Negroes and Mestizos and as superiors to the Indians." [28]

What special socioeconomic and occupational functions did the different socioethnic groups fulfill? Marxist authors, for whom the economic function is most important, and others have tried to identify the "castas" by function. It is, of course, clear that the peninsulars and criollos reserved for themselves the function of an aristocracy, leaving other tasks to the "plebs." [29] It may also be possible to discern a more detailed pattern. The peninsulars then appear as the bureaucrats and merchants par excellence, the criollos as the large landowners, the mestizos as the artisans, shopkeepers, and tenants, the mulattoes as urban manual workers, and, finally, the Indians as community peasants and manpower for different kinds of heavy, unskilled labor.[30] But such efforts to identify the "castas" according to social and economic functions necessarily imply generalizations that are bound, at times, to collide with historical evidence. Two examples will illustrate the bewilderingly complex social structure known as the Sociedad de Castas. The Indians who lived in the district of El Cercado in Lima possessed an impressive number of Negro slaves. On the other hand, Negro farmers in Alto Peru cultivated the land with the help of servile "Indios Yanaconas." [31] An interesting question, important if we are to meaningfully discuss the relationship between "casta" and socioeconomic function, is whether discriminatory wage rates were applied to members of different ethnic groups within the same occupation. But the little information that is available is contradictory.[32] It is obvious that much more research, pursued without bias, must be done before a more serious analysis of the relationship between ethnic group and the occupational and economic function can be undertaken.

[27] Miranda (1964), 157.

[28] Quoted by Rosenblat (1954), II, 165.

[29] Konetzke (1951b), 356–357.

[30] For similar efforts, see Chávez Orozco (1938), 24–25; Aguirre Beltrán (1946), 270–271. See also Bagú (1952), 53–55; Diffie (1945), 481–482; Othón de Mendizábal, IV (1946), 65.

[31] Harth-terré (1961); Wolff (1964), 185.

[32] Discrimination confirmed by Jara (1959), 74; denied by Harth-terré and Márquez Abanto (1962), 39 and *passim*.

In a way that was also natural in the Europe of those days, each of the "castas" was more or less distinguishable by its dress. The endless grievances of the authorities over the lower "castas' " excesses in dress have parallels in Europe. In 1681, the viceroy of Peru reported to his successor in detail what he had done to suppress the horrible "profanity in dressing of the Mulatto women of this City." [33] As early as 1665, the viceroy had forbidden Negro and mulatto women to wear any kind of silk under a penalty of having the dress confiscated, the first time it happened, and the second time, one hundred lashes with a whip and expulsion from the city of Lima.[34] The fair sex undoubtedly was especially active in the fights over dress, always taken very seriously by the authorities and public opinion of the time. In Venezuela the large mantillas of the white ladies gave rise to the famous "mantuano" as a designation for the elite, otherwise known, with an economic criterion, as "Los del Gran Cacao," referring to the cocoa plantations that they owned. In the seventeenth and eighteenth centuries, the Indians, by imitating the Spanish dress of the day, created the costumes that nowadays are considered to be typically "Indian." [35]

Discrimination and Intermarriage

The different "castas" were also separated by other means well known to any discriminatory society. The viceroy of Peru during the eighteenth century received visitors in two rooms, one for whites, another for Indians and mixed-bloods. In Caracas around 1800, the whites went to mass in the cathedral, the pardos to another church, and the Negroes to a third.[36] In accordance with a decision of the town council in 1723, the elementary school in Buenos Aires was strictly discrimi-

[33] *Memorias*, I (1859), 295. See also a royal decree of 1725, *CDFS*, III, 187.

[34] Muguburu, I (1928), 109. Detailed accounts of regional and social variations in dress in Juan and Ulloa (1768), I–II, *passim*. For a drastic example of how whites reacted against violations of dress "rules" by mulattoes, see Franco (1961), 166.

[35] Paradoxically, in Yucatán the "mestizo" dress is the popular dress as distinguished from the city type, "vestido." Redfield (1941), 64, 74–75. A Guatemalan friar in 1797 proposed that rural Indians and mestizos be "integrated" by having them adopt Spanish dress. Córdoba (1957).

[36] In the Cathedral of Cuzco there were three priests, two for Spaniards and one for Indians and slaves, a significant combination. Bueno (1951), 95.

natory. The teacher should teach only white and Indian children to read and write, whereas mestizos and mulattoes should be instructed only in Christian dogma, and the groups were to be kept apart when the teacher brought them to public functions.[37]

Discrimination was easily introduced by the many corporations within colonial society, such as the guilds and the *cofradías* (religious brotherhoods), the *consulados* (merchant associations), the universities, and the Church with all its branches. The more distinguished guilds, such as the silversmiths, were, of course, especially exclusivist in their admittance policy. On the other hand, the repugnance of the "Spaniards" to engage in manual work necessarily led to dark-skinned individuals penetrating into the guilds in spite of segregationist efforts.[38] In turn, the whites abstained from joining even guilds that had been socially acceptable, "choosing laziness," a Spanish traveler in late eighteenth-century Peru observes.[39] Sometimes, only people of African "blood" were excluded from membership. The Ordinances of the Potters in Mexico City in 1681 admitted Spaniards and mestizos but excluded Negroes and mulattoes from the guild.[40] A recent study of the carpenters and masons of Lima shows that even among the master craftsmen there were both mestizos and mulattoes.[41]

Sometimes, the corporations had to modify their efforts to enforce strict discrimination because of the opposition that they met, or for other reasons. When a "Patriotic Society" was formed in Buenos Aires in 1801, it was proposed that all foreigners, Negroes, mulattoes, zamboes, and mestizos be excluded, "because this Argentine society ought to be composed of men of honorable birth and good ways." But a little later it was conceded that naturalized foreigners and mestizos might be admitted in accordance with their legal status.[42] Nevertheless, it is obvious that exemption from pardo status by means of a Cédula de Gracias al Sacar, for instance, was not enough to overcome the obstacles created by socioethnic discrimination. A French traveler observed around 1800 that the only social effect of such a royal letter was that

[37] Rosenblat (1954), 136–137, 162; Konetzke (1946b), 232. A similar example from Cumaná, Venezuela in 1784 is in Leal (1963), 120.

[38] Carrera Stampa (1954), 223–243.

[39] Ruíz (1952), I, 25. See also a statement by Viceroy Revillagigedo (Jr.), *Instruciones*, II (1873), 52–53.

[40] Konetzke (1949b).

[41] Harth-terré and Márquez Abanto (1962), 18–19 and *passim*.

[42] Rosenblat (1954), II, 155.

the ladies of the pardo family in question now dared to put on a mantilla in Church, formerly the privilege of the whites.[43]

A concrete example will serve to illustrate this question. A pardo by the name of Diego Mejías Bejarano in Caracas obtained a Cédula de Gracias al Sacar in 1796. Seven years later he wanted to have his son enter the university, but this institution protested to the king that the presence of pardos would extinguish the splendor of letters, and shock those "justly proud of their pure Castilian blood." In 1805, the Crown overruled the university, but we still do not know if young Mejías was really allowed to enter. More than words would probably have been needed in this Spanish American "Ole Miss." [44] One document illustrates the attitude of the criollo elite especially well. I refer to the letter addressed by the town council of Caracas to the king in 1796 after it received a tariff for purchasing legal exemption from the status of pardo and of quinterón respectively. The aristocrats of Caracas declared:

> This transition . . . which is conceded in exchange for a small amount of money, is terrifying for the burghers and natives of America, because only they know, ever since their birth or by the experiences of many years, what an immense distance separates whites from *Pardos*, the advantage and superiority of the former and the baseness and subordination of the latter. Therefore, they would never dare to believe feasible the equality envisioned by the Royal decree. . . . How could the burghers and white natives of this Province possibly admit to their side . . . a Mulatto descended from their own or their fathers' slaves . . . a Mulatto, whose relatives find themselves in actual servitude, a Mulatto whose origin is stained by a long series of bastardies and turpitude. . . .

With a frankness that could not be greater, they concluded that the concept of pardo would never be allowed to disappear "despite all interference of law, privilege and grace." It seems paradoxical to find among the signatories, Carlos Palacios y Blanco, the uncle and tutor of Simón Bolívar.[45] The bulwark of prejudice was, at the same time, the cradle of liberty.

[43] Depons (1960), I, 120–121.

[44] Leal (1963), 326–332. Until 1822, "purity of the blood" was still required for matriculation at this university. Cf. Lanning (1955), 193–195. At the University of Córdoba, Argentina, the "castas" were excluded as late as 1844. Endrek (1966), 67.

[45] Blanco, I (1875), 267–268, 272.

As late as 1815, a relatively "liberal" European observer, José Ceballos, Captain General of Venezuela, was shocked to observe the extent of discrimination to which the so-called "castas" were subjected. They were not only excluded from "all municipal positions and other honorable occupations and distinctions, from entrance in some religious Congregations and brotherhoods," but "even from social contact with the white class. They could not approach the persons or houses of the whites without paying the same or greater respects than those paid to or due to public authority." [46]

Within the Society of Castes, with its prejudice and both legal and social forms of discrimination, many obstacles naturally opposed large-scale intermarriage. It was not exclusively a question of prejudice on the part of the whites. An Indian chronicler, Guamán Poma de Ayala, in the early seventeenth century admonished Indian caciques not to marry their daughters with lower class Indians or Spaniards "but only to their equals to produce people of good family [*buena casta*] in this kingdom." [47] The regulations of matrimony in Spanish America in 1778 reflect the same way of thinking from the European standpoint.[48] Without pretending to have carried out any systematic research on the subject, I may mention that a few samples taken by my wife and myself in ecclesiastical archives of Mexico and Guatemala indicate that, as might be expected, the majority of interracial marriages were concluded between members of more or less neighboring ethnic groups, as between castizo and Spaniard or mestizo and mulatto. But there were exceptions. Out of 186 weddings concluded in a chapel of the Cathedral of Oaxaca in 1756, at least half joined members of the same ethnic group and most of the rest were between ethnic "neighbors." But there were two between Spaniards and Indian women and five between pardos and Spanish women.[49] Of the weddings that took place in a chapel of the cathedral of Mexico City in 1810, most, 184, involved Spanish couples, but one joined a Spaniard with a Negro woman, seven, Spaniards with Indian women, and no less than sixteen, Indians

[46] King (1953), 531.

[47] Poma de Ayala (1944), 752/742.

[48] The town council of Mexico City wrote to the king in 1771 that the Spaniard who mixed with an Indian would find his sons without the honors due to Spaniards and also without the privileges of the Indians. Torres Quintero (1921), 10.

[49] Archivo del Sagrario, Oaxaca: *Libro de Matrimonios*, 1756.

with Spanish women. Rather surprising combinations appear, such as the following in Mexico City in 1756:

> Don Bernardo Marcos de Castro, Indian cacique and native of the City and Archdiocese of Manila in the Philippine islands and now resident at this Court . . . and Doña María Gertrudis de Rojas, Spanish and native of this City, legitimate daughter of Don José and Doña Rosa Clara Montes. . . .[50]

The Church also sanctioned another social tie of great importance for interethnic relations: *compadrazgo* (godparenthood). A case from the 1540's shows that the daughter of a Negro and his Indian wife was baptized in Lima with one Spaniard, one Genovese, a Negro woman, and an Indian woman as *padrinos* (godfathers).[51]

The ecclesiastical archives, until now little explored, hold considerable interest for those investigating social history and interethnic relations. But we cannot share the optimism of another student, who affirms that the priests were expert in ethnic classification and always sincere in their judgments.[52] If that were so, it would be easy and rewarding to compile statistics on the subject. But Richard Konetzke has published documentation that shows that the "racial" classification in the parish registers was simply based on the declaration of the parties and therefore not legally valid.[53] We have also observed how the terms employed by the priests varied from parish to parish and from time to time.

Though intermarriage always existed, its frequency seems to have increased toward the end of the colonial period. It was undoubtedly the greater pressure exercised by a better organized Church that led to the legitimation of many existing unions. A Mexican scholar presents a list of twenty Spaniards who, under the threat of being deprived of absolution, married Negro and mulatto slaves and free women in Puebla between 1690 and 1695.[54] But we should keep in mind that during the eighteenth century in particular, both the culture and the wealth of

[50] Archivo del Sagrario Metropolitano, Mexico City: *Libro de matrimonios de españoles*, vol. 41 (1810–1811); *Libro de Amonestaciones de los de color quebrado*, 1756–1757, 13 v. Both in Mexico and Peru the presence of a number of Asiatics who arrived with the Manila galleon can be noticed. Several "Indios chinos" and "Japoneses" were active as artisans and workers in Lima between 1595 and 1610. Harth-terré and Márquez Abanto (1962), 89–90.

[51] Harth-terré (1962), 81–82.

[52] Roncal (1944), 532.

[53] Konetzke (1946a).

[54] Aguirre Beltrán (1946), 252–253.

the intermediate groups in colonial society increased. For the people belonging to this intermediate stratum, marriage became the natural form of union. Such marriage was likely often to unite members of neighboring "castas" such as castizo and mestizo or mestizo and mulatto. This explains the apparent contradiction during the eighteenth century between, on the one hand, increased prejudice among the white elite, and, on the other, increasingly frequent intermarriage. In fact, it was the advance and expansion of the intermediate groups that essentially motivated the increased exclusivism displayed by the criollo elite.[55]

A vivid illustration for our discussion of intermarriage, with all its contradictions, is the following story from New Granada (the present Colombia), told by an eighteenth-century missionary. Don Rodrigo, son of a criollo landowner, had lived with a mulatto woman for nine years and had four children by her. He now wanted to marry her. In vain the good friar admonished him that such a marriage often turned love into abhorrence and warned him of his father's ire and the stain on his pure blood. But finally the friar gave up and married the two. Foolishly enough, Don Rodrigo gave the news to his father in person. He barely escaped two shots from his gun. But, if we can trust the friar, there was no happy ending — as we see it. Don Rodrigo came to loathe his poor wife and made peace with his irate father. Maybe this saved him from being disinherited.[56]

Illegitimacy probably continued to attach to most children of mixed origin born in Spanish America.[57] In all multiracial societies in which

[55] According to Depons (1960), I, 121–123, very few high-class criollos married pardas, whereas the combination more frequently occurred with poor criollos and Canarians (until a legal restriction was issued in 1785). Criollo girls, once abandoned by their mothers for being fruits of illicit relationships, often married pardos, he adds.

[56] Santa Gertrudis (1956), I, 333–335, 346, 403–404.

[57] According to Borah & Cook (1966), 262–264, "most of the people (in colonial Mexico) did marry in accordance with church requirements." Their statement is based on parish registers in Mixteca Alta (Oaxaca) and applies particularly to the Indians. They admit that "church and state were far less able to impose official morality" in districts with mixed population, but state that even in Antequera, a town with mixed population, the majority did get married (on the basis of data from 1777). Carmagnani (1963), 30, shows that only a fourth of the children in El Norte Chico, Chile, between 1690 and 1800 were illegitimate, but it is difficult to say if this sample is representative or not. Compare Carmagnani & Klein (1965), tables V–VIII. More research is needed on the frequency of illegitimacy in colonial Latin America. It is particularly interesting because of the sad conditions in this respect in Latin America today.

discrimination is practiced, it is well known that women of "inferior" race prefer concubinage with a man of the "superior" race to marriage with a member of their own race. This is explicitly confirmed in eighteenth-century Quito and Peru by traveler Antonio de Ulloa, who, though he noticed that public prostitution was absent, emphasized the willingness of dark-skinned women to engage in concubinage as soon as they were assured of some security or permanency in the relationship. Thus the continued illegitimacy of a great many people of mixed origin helped to maintain and strengthen existing prejudice against them; a vicious circle.[58]

The Society of Castes Crumbles

The Society of Castes was being undermined by the very process that had helped to bring it into being, miscegenation. Once a multiracial terminology had been adopted, it simply became impossible to apply any universally valid and strict criterion for classifying an increasingly mixed population. As early as 1646, Chilean chronicler Alonso de Ovalle observed that there was no mark "to distinguish [the mestizo] from the pure Spaniard, except the hair which is not modified for two or three generations. Otherwise, there is no difference, not in the features of the face, nor in the form of the body or in the way of speaking and of pronunciation." Juan and Ulloa report from Quito that there were many mestizos who ". . . from the advantage of a fresh complexion, appear to be Spaniards more than those who are so in reality. . . ." [59] Nor was the distance great between Indian and mestizo, so that passing from one category to the other might be relatively easy.[60] Concolorcorvo, a keen and somewhat mysterious traveler in the 1770's, observed that "the Indian is not distinct from the Spaniard in the shape of the face. When one of them enters the service of one of us [i.e., the whites] who treats him with charity, then his first measure is to teach the Indian cleanliness, to wash his face, to comb his hair, to cut his nails. When this is done and he is clad in a clean shirt, the Indian, though otherwise maintaining his own dress, passes as Cholo;

[58] Juan and Ulloa (1953), 384–386.
[59] Ovalle (1888), 166; Juan and Ulloa (1768), I, 279. Their own criteria for recognizing mestizos are not very convincing.
[60] A good example of how a person might be classified around 1600 is given by Jara (1959), 60: ". . . Mestizo woman to judge from how she looked and what she said, but in Indian dress. . . ."

that is, as somebody who has some Mestizo admixture. If his service is of use to the Spaniard, he gets a [Spanish] dress and shoes are put on his feet. Within a couple of months he is a mestizo by name." [61] If we consider the testimonies of Ovalle, Ulloa, and Concolorcorvo, how would it be feasible to distinguish between lobos, moriscos, and coyotes? Necessarily, both priests and authorities had to trust the declarations of the interested parties. Because of the colonial society's discriminatory character, the result had to be that the individual tried to pass from a more modest and "obscure" category to a more "bright" and superior one.[62] Two examples taken from tax lists from New Spain will illustrate:

Manuel Hilario López, Spaniard as he says but of very suspect color
. . . Juan Antonio Mendoza, Castizo of obscure skin [63]

Expressions such as "taken for Spaniard" or "reputed to be Spanish" abound in contemporary documentation. Faced with this situation, civil servants became confused and sometimes desperate. Juan Antonio de Areche, then Crown attorney of the audiencia of Mexico, wrote to the viceroy in 1770:

The liberty with which the plebs have been allowed to choose the class they prefer, insofar as their color permits, has stained the class of natives as well as that of Spaniards. They very often join the one or the other as it suits them or as they need to. . . . A Mulatto, for instance, whose color helps him somewhat to hide in another "casta," says, according to his whims, that he is Indian to enjoy the privileges as such and pay less tribute, though this seldom occurs, or, more frequently, that he is Spaniard, Castizo or Mestizo, and then he does not pay any [tribute] at all. . . .[64]

As noticed by Areche, passing was not necessarily a question of upward mobility within the social structure. Whereas the Indian might wish to pass for a mestizo in order to escape paying tribute, the mestizo might find it convenient, in certain cases, to present himself as an Indian to

[61] Concolorcorvo (1942), 328–329. This definition of the transitory concept of *cholo* is much better than any to be found in the monograph on this topic by Varallanos (1962). See also Kubler (1952), 36–37.

[62] This was also the conclusion of Francisco de Miranda, the famous "Precursor," in an account written in 1805. Miranda (1950), XXI, 248.

[63] Aguirre Beltrán (1946), 273–274.

[64] MS. 151, Mendel Collection, Lilly Library, University of Indiana, Bloomington, Ind.

escape the jurisdiction of the Inquisition. The resigned attitude of the authorities toward the end of the colonial era is well expressed in the following report from an administrator in New Spain:

> Nobody dares to classify the "castas." This would imply the gathering of odious information and, if rigorously done, very dark stains already erased by time would be uncovered in well-accepted families. . . . I have indicated the "castas" as Spaniard, Castizo, Mestizo, Pardo accord‌ing to the declarations of the citizens themselves, though some made me suspect that they were not telling the truth. . . .[65]

It is necessary to keep these circumstances well in mind whenever the demographic material of the time is used in studying ethnic groups.[66] The possibility of "passing" also explains the relative facility with which limited vertical social mobility evidently functioned during the last century of colonial rule within the "pigmentocracy." At that time, as we shall see, it had become nearly impossible to determine ra‌cial classification within the rural population of Spanish America. This was especially true of the proletariat who lived within the large hacien‌das. But, by and large, the Society of Castes, with its legal sanction and deep roots in social attitudes and values, continued to form the basis of social stratification until the very end of the colonial era, whereas the class system, in the words of Lyle McAlister, was only "an incipient situation." [67] Probably the best proof is provided by the serious tensions and frustrations engendered by the discrimination proper of the Society of Castes and eloquently manifested in the long wars of emancipation.

Race and Society in Brazil

The society of colonial Portuguese America had much in common with that of Spanish America, but it gives the impression of having been more fluid and less strictly regulated. Also, the ethnic terminology current in Brazil was more vague. *Mameluco* was applied to the mes‌tizo, but *mestiço* was also used for the Portuguese-Indian mixture. "Mestiço" might also refer, however, to mulattoes. *Caboclo* applied to

[65] Aguirre Beltrán (1946), 274. Even the basic terms were used somewhat vaguely at times. "Mulatto," as used by the authorities in El Salvador in the census of 1807, seems to have included mestizos as well. Barón Castro (1942), 254–256.

[66] Mörner (1966c), 21–22. Cf. Borah in *IPGH* (1961), 63–73.

[67] McAlister (1963), 362–363.

mestizos as well as acculturated Indians. "Pardo" could be used about practically any person of color.[68]

Undoubtedly, slavery was much more significant in Brazilian than in Spanish American society. Most Indians were subjected to a more or less slavocratic regime, at least until their legal emancipation in the 1750's. As historian Caio Prado Júnior aptly expressed it, slavery, and its two main functions, exploitation of manual work and sexual exploitation, tends to brutalize and simplify human relations. Since the only organized sector of colonial society was based on slavery, it is clear why a more comprehensive and complex superstructure was lacking. The dichotomy of masters and slaves prevailed. The situation was even worse, Prado argues, in the sector that remained outside slavery. "Non-organization was there the rule." [69] An abnormally high percentage of the free population of Brazil, being unable or unwilling to compete with the enslaved manpower, lived more or less as vagabonds in the marginal zone of society. This phenomenon has been called *vadiagem* or *caboclização*. There can be no doubt that miscegenation has been especially profound and widespread within this amorphous human mass, though, for obvious reasons, available historical documentation will hardly permit a closer study of the process.

Gilberto Freyre's descriptions of race relations in another environment, that of the large sugar plantations of the northeast, have come to be universally known and widely admired.[70] Therefore, we do not have to take up the subject here, but one circumstance will help in evaluating Freyre's interpretation. The Negro and mulatto slaves described by the famous sociologist of Pernambuco were usually domestics, and therefore privileged in comparison to the field hands who formed the bulk of the human property. Whereas Freyre and others emphasize how valuable was the African contribution to acculturation, the coldly materialistic Caio Prado expresses the opinion that because slavery required only brute force and sexual acceptance, the African contribution to Brazilian civilization had to be "almost zero." [71] Probably, the historical truth lies somewhere between these extreme positions.

Indian slavery in Maranhão is relatively well known, mainly thanks

[68] Boxer (1963), 87.
[69] Prado (1961), 341–343.
[70] Especially Freyre (1950), the first edition of which appeared in 1933.
[71] Prado (1961), 270. Boxer (1963), 104–110, summarizes a very interesting Portuguese treatise on slavery from 1764.

to the evidence supplied by the missionaries, even though this was necessarily biased. In the south of Brazil, from São Paulo downward, Indian slavery also provided a basis for the process of miscegenation, that is, for society itself. The daring mamelucos were the offspring of enslaved Indian women and, at the same time, hunters of Indians themselves. The patriarchal family of the high plateau of São Paulo comprised a numerous progeny of mixed and illegitimate birth.[72] Referring especially to the later period of mameluco or *bandeirante* expansion, Cassiano Ricardo affirms that the African element was of great importance in this expansion and, consequently, also in the miscegenation that accompanied the advance.[73]

The presence of a numerous Negro slave population in the south of Brazil is confirmed by the census taken in 1776 and by other coeval documentation. Almost a third of the population of Rio Grande do Sul were Negro slaves. In Minas Gerais, half the population were classified as Negroes, a fourth as whites, and another fourth as pardos. As we have already pointed out, however, the classification is extremely vague. In São Paulo, where more than half the population were recorded as whites, the Indian Tupí language remained the mother tongue of most inhabitants.[74]

It might seem unlikely that such a fluid society could provide a basis for socioracial prejudice, and many students have denied that it did. But even Freyre admits that fathers of white girls were faced with only two alternatives: send the daughter to a convent or find a "pure" white husband for her, if possible a peninsular. To have a white wife was a symbol of prestige and she had to be efficiently watched over.[75] It is clear that, from 1755 onward, the Crown's policy of fomenting Indian-Portuguese intermarriage met with little sympathy.[76] The haughty and exclusivist attitude of the "whites" had nothing to do, of course, with their sexual habits. Mulatto girls were the favorite concubines, as a popular proverb put it: "E a mulata que é mulher!" (The mulatto girl is *the* woman!) Another often quoted proverb defined Brazil as a hell for Negroes, a purgatory for whites, and a paradise for mulattoes. But the social status of mulattoes was rather far from being

[72] An interesting account, based on contemporary inventories and wills in Machado (1953), 158–165.

[73] Ricardo (1942), II.

[74] Alden (1963), 66; Rosenblat (1954), II, 104.

[75] Freyre (1950).

[76] Boxer (1963), 199.

paradisiac. Because of their stigmas of slavery and illegitimacy, the pardos were subjected to forms of social discrimination beyond that already imposed by law. An effort to "integrate" the units of militia in the ethnic sense failed conspicuously during the 1730's. The *irmandades* (counterparts of Spanish American *cofradías*) maintained a policy of racial exclusivism.[77]

Because of the fluidity of Brazilian colonial society, the phenomenon of "passing" must have been even more frequent there than in Spanish America. A traveler gives us an amusing example from the early nineteenth century. When asking somebody if a certain local administrator, *Capitão-mor*, was a mulatto, he got the answer: "He used to be, but is no longer." When the traveler showed his bewilderment, the other exclaimed: "But, sir, could a Capitão-mor possibly be a mulatto?" [78] Obviously, among the mixed-bloods, one's darker or brighter complexion was of great importance. The name *preto* or Negro came to be full of contempt.[79] The phenotype of the child born in concubinage between master and slave often decided whether this mulatto would be manumitted or not.[80]

Whatever the attitude of the superior strata toward miscegenation, nothing could have stopped or even slowed it down in the Brazilian environment. It seems as if in Brazil there was a lack of white women for much longer than in Spanish America.[81] It is not in any way necessary to seek the reason for widespread miscegenation in Brazil in the preference for dark women among the Portuguese or the tolerance of Portuguese racial policy. Essentially, total race mixture resulted from the country's peculiarity in colonization and economy: the necessarily small number of Portuguese colonizers, the labor requirements of the sugar economy, and the mining boom around 1700 which suddenly attracted great numbers of male immigrants. Both slavery and vagrancy provided ideal conditions for large-scale promiscuity.

[77] Boxer (1962), 15, 142, and *passim*; (1963), 119–120.
[78] Ianni (1962), 263, quoting J. M. Rugendas.
[79] Prado (1961), 271–272.
[80] Cf. Hutchinson (1957), 99.
[81] Boxer (1962), 164–165; Calmon (1937), I, 75–76.

"Negro man and Indian woman sire Lobo." Courtesy of *Museo de América, Madrid.*

VI

Revolt of the Man with Dark Skin

Mestizo Frustration and Vagrancy

The psychological reactions of the people of mixed origin to the discriminatory conditions imposed by the Society of Castes were complex. Eric Wolf has excellently depicted the type of clever and pliable mestizo, diligent intermediary for all the subtle transactions required within society but always pursuing ambitions of his own at the same time.[1] But there was also a frustrated type of mestizo. At times, this frustration expressed itself in escapism; at times, in aggression. Sergio Bagú writes that the mestizo of the colonial period, who "was not allocated any place within the economic structure, also lacked an allocation in the social structure because, not being Negro or Indian, he tried to be white without success. Colonial society placed him between two fires, creating resentment in him. In addition, he received neither work, nor education." [2]

As early as the sixteenth century, vagrancy had grown inordinately, the vagabonds (*vagos* in Spanish; *vadios* in Portuguese) being mainly mestizos and mulattoes. The authorities, the peninsulars and criollos, and the Indians, all were terrified to see the virulence of the phenomenon. Their repugnance strengthened their prejudice, which, in turn, added to the frustration on which vagrancy was nurtured. "So-

[1] Wolf (1962), ch. XI.
[2] Bagú (1952), 113.

ciety suffers for being crowded with lost and vagrant people who do not apply themselves to work, nor is there any to be found, and they cause injury and insolence to both natives and Spaniards. They always escape because the country is vast . . . ," Viceroy Luis de Velasco of New Spain reported in 1593.[3] Both the Crown and local authorities tenaciously tried to reduce vagrancy and to prevent the vagrants from abusing the Indians. The residential separation policy in Spanish America was partly dictated by this aim. As the long colonial period continued, vagrancy seemed to diminish, relatively if not absolutely. However this may have been, it was probably not reduced by the authorities' efforts but rather because vagrants were attracted by the surplus land left uncultivated by a declining Indian population. Very much against the intentions of the Crown, many former vagrants settled down among the Indians to cultivate their land. Nevertheless, Spanish America and Brazil always included a great many unemployed and vagrant individuals.

This sector absorbed elements of different ethnic backgrounds. The motivation of Negro and mulatto slaves to try to escape from a society that repressed them without mercy was, of course, particularly strong. At times, their violent rebellions, though always suppressed, facilitated mass desertions. These *Negros cimarrones* especially worried the authorities, since the loss of slaves was of direct economic importance and because the Negroes often engaged in banditry. The measures taken by the authorities against the cimarrones were usually cruel, but far from efficient.[4] The deserters, naturally enough, dared to settle only in villages rather far from Spanish or Portuguese settlements. These centers of African population and resistance were called *palenques* or *cumbes* in Spanish America, *quilombos* in Brazil. A large-scale military campaign was required to destroy the so-called *Quilombo dos Palmares* in Brazil, the "Negro Troy," toward the end of the seventeenth century. If such refuges were not destroyed, they continued to attract growing numbers of slaves from the plantations.[5] Necessarily, the flight

[3] Martin (1957), 106. That vagrancy also existed among the Indians should also be noticed. In Peru the yanaconas were a rootless, floating proletariat. *HSAI*, II, 377–379.

[4] Martin (1957), 122–124; Saco (1938), II, *passim*; Guillot (1961), 66–71 and *passim*; Acosta Saignes (1961).

[5] Carneiro (1958), 14–17, emphasizes that the organizers of the quilombos probably were newcomers from Africa and that the background from which these refugee colonies emerged was always "a situation of local economic difficulties that led to a certain laxity in slave discipline." See also Jaramillo Uribe (1963), 42–50; Davidson (1966).

of Negro slaves into remote areas extended miscegenation, in the first place with Indian women. The extraordinarily warlike tribes of zamboes in the district of Esmeraldas in the jurisdiction of the audiencia of Quito and those on the Mosquito Coast in Nicaragua were the products of this kind of mestizaje. But Negro and zambo attackers also brought back white and mestizo women from their raids. A missionary who roamed around in the wild inlands of Cartagena in New Granada in the late eighteenth century has preserved a few violent, colorful accounts of women kidnapped and raped by the lawless zamboes.[6]

In other regions, the mestizos were predominant among the vagrants. Their marginal existence was formed by the geoeconomic environment, however, not by the ethnic composition of the vagrants. This is true, for instance, of the gauchos of Río de la Plata, "a case of Mestizaje of free herdsmen," as Carlos Rama has put it.[7] It was the abundance of wild cattle, the famous *vaquerías*, that provided the gauchos with their subsistence and helped to shape their life. Even at the beginning of the seventeenth century, documents from Río de la Plata began to mention those "lost young men," who, brought up in the small urban centers of the region, went "to hunt and live among the Indians, copying their customs and defects." [8] From this time onward, it is possible to follow these vagrants on horseback through their occasional contacts with society as temporary cattle hands or as smugglers, though the first known mention of the word "gaucho" dates only from 1774.[9] The sexual life of the gauchos was clearly restricted because women, of whatever skin color, were scarce in the immense plains of the pampas. Thus a contemporary observer notices that in the late eighteenth century many women lived in simple huts near the town of San Nicolás, each of them satisfying the needs of several gauchos and taking care of their children. This form of polyandry, called *aparcería*, was based on mutual agreement among the men frequenting the same woman.[10] The alternative to this arrangement was bloody fights over the women. A woman told a Spanish traveler that ten years earlier she

    [6] Palacios de la Vega (1955), 38ff.
    [7] *IPGH* (1961), 94.
    [8] Coni (1945), 45–52.
    [9] Rodríguez Molas (1964), 81–82, rectifies the date given by Coni: 1790. The etymology of the word "gaucho" is controversial. According to Assunçao (1963), 369–536, it derives either from *guacho*, meaning "illegitimate," "orphan," or is related to *gauche* (Provençal), meaning "twisted," "astray," "erring."
    [10] Coni (1945), 70.

had been kidnapped by a certain Cuenca but that he was killed by another gaucho who, in turn, succumbed to a third man, who now possessed her.[11] That the women of the gauchos belonged to different ethnic groups is obvious. During the eighteenth century, a more rational form of exploitation of the cattle resources, the *estancias*, was extended, increasing the pressure of society on the gauchos. A Spanish civil servant reported in 1790 that the poor peasants of Banda Oriental, the present Uruguay, were really forced "to do without license what others do with doubtful rights, that is to slaughter cattle to right and left in order to draw off the hides, which they bring to rich Spaniards and Portuguese who only pay them a trifle for [these hides]." [12] But it was only by the middle of the nineteenth century that the gauchos met their destiny, eliminated by barbed wire, colonization by European immigrants, and modern cattle breeding. When the great epic of Martín Fierro was published in 1872, the time had come for the historic gaucho to disappear and make room for the gaucho myth.

Parallel geoeconomic conditions produced another, similar marginal group, the llanero of the plains along the Orinoco river. Ethnically, the llaneros held a greater percentage of African blood. A recent study shows that in Chile vagrancy was most frequent in the cattle region along the southern frontier. Like the gauchos and llaneros, the Chilean vagrants on horseback were active in the wars of emancipation, rallying around leaders of their own choice.[13] In Mexico, the region called El Bajío was much more integrated with society than either the pampas or the llanos, but its cattle breeding and mining economy likewise attracted unstable and adventurous elements. It was precisely there that the popular revolt of Allende and Father Hidalgo broke out in 1810.[14]

Indian and Mestizo Revolts and the Wars of Emancipation

Within the colonial society, the resentment and aggression of the oppressed masses manifested themselves from time to time in rebellions and riots.[15] Indian uprisings were in fact usual, and most were quite

[11] Azara (1943), 202–203.
[12] Rodríguez Molas (1964), 84.
[13] Góngora (1966).
[14] W. Jiménez Moreno in *IPGH* (1961), 84; Wolf (1957).
[15] According to Guthrie (1945), one of the principal causes of the popular uprisings in Mexico City in 1624 and 1692 was social inequality, "produced by sharply marked class distinctions which were mainly racial."

easy to put down. But one large-scale rebellion for a moment seemed to really threaten Spanish domination, that of the Andean Indians under Tupac Amaru in 1780 and 1781. Though the leader was a mestizo, strictly speaking, he considered himself a successor of the Incas and seems to have dreamt of re-establishing their empire. In any case, the rebellion became increasingly Indian, causing the entire non-Indian population to close ranks in order to defend the regime. This proved fatal for the rebels.[16]

The uprisings of mestizos were usually more moderate, directed as they were against some new tax or other unpopular administrative measure. Even so, they often reflected deep hatred between mestizos and whites.[17] Many have evaluated the mestizo uprisings as conscientious expressions of patriotism, because the ringleaders usually were cruelly put to death as traitors, but this interpretation is misleading. Following the disorders caused by the zambo contrabandist Andresote in Venezuela, between 1730 and 1733, many men of color were executed, whereas some large landowners, who were also compromised, escaped punishment.[18] From the ideological point of view, only the rebellions of the so-called *comuneros* of Paraguay in the 1720's and 1730's and the comunero movement in New Granada during the 1780's deserve real interest. In New Granada, the rebellion of the mestizo comuneros coincided with an Indian uprising headed by Ambrosio Pisco. But the alliance between the two probably weakened rather than strengthened the comunero rebellion because of the tensions it created.[19]

In one way or another faint echoes of the French revolution, or, rather, its sequel in Haiti, reached the Spanish American masses. In Coro, Venezuela, José Leonardo Chirino, a free zambo, made himself leader of a slave uprising with the aim of introducing "the law of the French." He probably meant wholesale slaughter of the whites, but the result of the revolt was the opposite.[20]

We must emphasize, however, that the emancipation movement in Spanish America, anticipated by a great many crushed conspiracies, was

[16] The literature on Tupac Amaru is vast but mediocre. A reference to Lewin (1943) may suffice here.

[17] A leader of the mestizo mutiny in Peru in 1567 declared that "the meanest Mestizo is better than the best Spaniard." López Martínez (1965).

[18] Felice Cardot (1952).

[19] Henao and Arrubla (1938), 168–169. See also Lewin (1943), 673–717, on the repercussions of the Peruvian rebellion in New Granada and Venezuela.

[20] Arcaya (1949).

above all the work of the criollo elite, set in motion when the Napoleonic invasion of Spain had brought about a series of disruptive events. The only exceptions of any importance were the popular rebellions in New Spain, led by the two parish priests, Hidalgo and Morelos, and defeated with the help of frightened criollos. In Brazil, socioracial tensions on the eve of emancipation had created a dangerous situation. The abortive movement of 1798, known as the "Inconfidencia" of Bahía, apparently was directed by mulattoes of modest origin. In Bahía, there were also frequent uprisings of slaves (no fewer than eight between 1807 and 1835).[21] But, as we know, Brazil obtained independence in an extraordinarily tranquil way, thanks to fortunate circumstances that preserved the monarchy. Hence, no events were explosive enough to release a large-scale socioracial struggle.

Humiliations suffered by individuals under the Society of Castes helped to create revolutionaries. The great example is Francisco Javier Eugenio de Espejo, the zambo intellectual of Quito, whose tragic life was a daring challenge to a society based on privilege and social inequality.[22] But we must also realize that by far the majority of single conspirators and revolutionaries were criollos. Espejo's example shows how difficult it was for one of the disdained castas to obtain the education required to create an "enlightened" revolutionary.

The wars of emancipation were civil wars. Both sides drafted Indians, Negroes, and castas to do a great part of the fighting. Most men in the loyalist army in Peru and Alto Peru, the present Bolivia, were Indians. Between 30 and 40 per cent of the patriot army that General San Martín brought across the Andes to liberate Chile seem to have been Negroes.[23] For all their bravery, these fighting men of color were pawns, driven on by interests more or less alien to their own.

But during the wars there were occasions when all the tensions and hatreds, bottled up under the Society of Castes, threatened to explode, bringing on a socioracial struggle. Let us first look at Venezuela. In 1813, as is well known, two Spanish officers, Tomás Boves and Francisco Morales, strove to incite the llaneros against the criollo rebels, inaugurating the most savage phase of the struggle. "We are going to

[21] Prado (1961), 367, believes that "the sinew of the projected uprising was the difference of castes, a revolt against color prejudice." See also Carneiro (1964), 31.

[22] Picón-Salas (1963), 153. Another example is the Peruvian poet and naturalist José Manuel Valdés, a mulatto. Romero (1942).

[23] Masini (1962).

fall into the hands of the Negroes. May God grant that I am mistaken!", one of the criollo leaders wrote in anguish to his wife,[24] darkly foreshadowing racial warfare. And Archbishop Coll y Prat reported to Madrid about the 1,500 "Zamboes and Mulattoes," who entered Caracas proclaiming "general slaughter of the whites." [25] In spite of everything, it seems that the fears as well as the many descriptions of the cruelty of Boves and his men were somewhat exaggerated.[26] We should not forget that history was written by the victors. In 1817, Bolívar succeeded in persuading the new llanero chieftain, José Antonio Paez, to join the patriots instead. From that moment, the llaneros' savage heroism was in the service of the criollo revolutionaries. In the same year, Bolívar caused sensation when he had one of his best generals, Manuel Piar, executed for insubordination. It is impossible to escape the impression that Piar was so harshly punished because he was a mulatto. Bolívar wrote to a friend that Piar had started "to provoke the war of colors." [27] In fact, the loyalist generals harbored the same fear. Captain General Francisco Montalvo wrote to the Spanish government in 1814 that Boves had been able to rally between ten and twelve thousand "Zamboes and Mulattoes who now fight to destroy the white Criollos, their masters, because of the community of interests [with us] that they find in this. It will not take long before they start to destroy the white Europeans, who are also their masters, and whose death will give them the same benefit as that of the former." [28] A prophesy that proved to be true! The new general-in-chief of the loyalists, Pablo Morillo, in 1817 sent a very courageous colored officer to Spain explicitly because he had proved to be "a stalwart foe of all whites. He has also commanded people of his own color and exercises too much influence over them. . . ." [29] We may conclude that the risk of a clear socioracial struggle in Venezuela, already a battleground for years, was removed because neither patriot nor loyalist commanders wanted this kind of struggle.

[24] Letter by Martín Tovar Ponte, July 15, 1813, in *Epistolario*, II, (1960), 380. In his London exile, Francisco de Miranda expressed in 1809 his fears for "the fury of Mulattoes and Negroes." Miranda (1950), XXII, 350.

[25] Coll y Prat (1960), 298–299.

[26] For a less emotional appreciation of Boves, see Carrera Damas (1964).

[27] Bolívar to Luis López Méndez, November 11, 1817, in Lecuna, *Cartas*, I, 117. Cf. Masur (1948), 305–311. See also Griffin (1962), 57.

[28] Quoted by Vallenilla Lanz (1961), 96.

[29] *Ibid.*, 97–98.

In Mexico, it is well known that, incited by the fiery speeches of Miguel de Hidalgo, the Indian hordes now and then took bloody revenge on the whites, as in the horrible massacre of the public granary of Granaditas in Guanajuato. When the criollos realized that the war cry of "Death to the Gachupines," the invective for peninsulars, included themselves as well, they did not hestitate to help suppress the uprising. But it is most interesting that José María Morelos, at first the principal aide of, and thereafter successor to Hidalgo, and a mestizo or "moreno" himself, did intervene as soon as he considered a race war to be clearly imminent. By a decree issued in Tecpán on October 13, 1811, Morelos declared that:

> . . . our system is only intended to invest the political and military government that now resides in the Europeans, in the Criollos instead . . . and that consequently there be no distinction of [racial] qualities but that we should all call ourselves Americans . . . from which it follows that everybody ought to know that there is no reason for those who used to be called "Castas" to try to destroy each other, for whites to fight Negroes, or Negroes to fight natives. . . . As the whites are the first representatives of the Kingdom and the first to take up arms in defense of the people and the other "castes" . . . the whites, by virtue of these merits, should deserve our gratitude and not the hatred that one has tried to instil against them. . . .

To underline his words, Father Morelos had the two patriot leaders, whose behavior had directly provoked the decree, executed.[30]

Legal Discrimination Ends

The attitude of the criollo elite was strikingly ambivalent when criollos had to face the socioracial consequences of the very movement they had brought into being. On the one side were their fears, as we have already illustrated, and their desire to maintain their privileged position; on the other, was the influence exercised over them by the equalitarian ideas of the French revolution. In Venezuela, the first Spanish American nation to declare its independence, the fathers of the constitution of 1811, after much debating, prohibited the importation of slaves, made the Indian equal with other citizens, and abolished "the ancient laws that imposed civil degradation on part of the free population of Venezuela hitherto known under the name of Pardos. They are to enjoy the natural and civil reputation and to re-

[30] González del Cossío (1958), 26; Chávez (1957), 48–52.

cover the inalienable rights that correspond to them as to all other citizens." [31] Other early consitutions of the new Spanish American republics granted citizenship to all those born in the country in question, without explicitly referring to previous discrimination. In Mexico, Morelos, then acting in the name of Hidalgo, prohibited the use of labels such as Indian, mulatto, and casta in November, 1810.[32]

Hence, political emancipation tangibly affected every parish in the immense region, when one day the traditional classification into ethnic groups suddenly was discontinued. Let us take as an example an entry found in the register of marriages in one of the churches of Mexico City in 1822:

> By order of the Superior government a proclamation was made public on the 14th of this month of January ordering that the qualities of Spaniards, Indians, Mulattoes, etc. no longer be specified in parish registers, but that everybody receive the qualification of American, and this order will be carried out from today onwards. . . .[33]

Applying the new equalitarian concept did not always prove easy. High authorities themselves sometimes found it difficult to abandon the word "Indian," even in their decrees. For some time, the courts were reluctant to cease treating the Indians as legal minors.[34] Nevertheless, legal and administrative equalization was an innovation of great importance. No longer did prejudice and different forms of socioracial discrimination find endorsement in legislation. On the other hand, the indigenous population did not find in the new legislation the special protection that it often required.

While we are considering constitutionalism and civil rights for the dark-skinned, we should examine briefly the Liberal Assembly at Cadiz, Spain, which was to produce the Constitution of 1812, even though that constitution was doomed to a short life. Here the antidiscriminatory attitude of the Spanish American deputies was intimately related to the problem of the popular basis of constitutional monarchy.[35] By

[31] Pensamiento (1961), V, 93.

[32] González del Cossío (1958), 23. According to González Navarro (1955), Hidalgo himself favored criollo rather than Indian interests, but the behavior of his Indian followers scared the criollos.

[33] Archives of the parish of Santa Catarina, Mexico City: *Libro de matrimonios*, 1810–1822.

[34] Bushnell (1954), 173, 182. The authorities "even found it hard to eschew the word *salvaje*." On the treatment of Indians as legal minors, see González del Cossío (1958), 168.

[35] We follow here the excellent account by King (1953b).

virtue of an equalitarian representative system, the overseas possessions with their 15 or 16 million inhabitants would necessarily dominate a common parliament, since Spain held only 10 or 11 million people. The "liberal" Spanish deputies then found a means of reducing the American basis by appealing to the divisions dictated by the Society of Castes. However prejudiced they were personally on race and class questions, the Spanish American deputies offered determined resistance. At first, the peninsulars tried to exclude the Indians, but in this respect the Laws of the Indies were too openly in favor of the natives, so they had to give way. Then they concentrated on trying to exclude those of African blood. Despite rather loud opposition by the Americans, they succeeded. A clever compromise, suggested by a Peruvian, would have had the castas enjoy suffrage but not be eligible; it, too was rejected. By a formula as astute as it was entangled, the constitution came to state that the "basis of national representation . . . is the population composed by the natives who on both sides derive from the Spanish dominions." But the individual possibility of "passing" allowed already by the Cédulas de Gracias al Sacar was not annulled, because another paragraph stated:

> For those Spaniards who on either side are reputed [!] to originate from Africa, the door of virtue and merits remains open to become citizens. Consequently, the Cortes [the Spanish parliament] will grant letters of citizenship to those who render qualified services to the Fatherland, to those distinguished by their talent, application and conduct, granted that they are born in legitimate marriage of free parents, that they are married to a free woman . . . and that they exercise some profession, office or useful industrial occupation with capital of their own.[36]

A decree of 1812 also opened the doors of universities, seminaries, and the priesthood to the pardos, but with reservations that reduced considerably the value of the decree.[37] Under these circumstances, the triumph won at Cadiz by the peninsular "liberals" only served to provide patriot propaganda with ammunition.[38] And, after Ferdinand VII

[36] Pensamiento (1961), V, 296–297, 299.
[37] King (1953a), 529.
[38] In 1814, the deputies at the Cadiz assembly made an amusing propagandistic gesture when they ceded their allowances for one day to provide a dowry "for the first Indian woman to marry a European Spaniard in the first place of the parts now in rebellion that gives the Nation the consolation of returning to it on account of the coming of Don Ferdinand VII." Ots Capdequí (1958), 366.

returned from French captivity, the restricted liberalism initiated by the Constitution of 1812 also disappeared. Intelligent loyalist commanders realized the adverse psychological effect produced by the Spanish government's indifference toward socioracial issues. The captain general of Venezuela, now José Ceballos, wrote to the king in 1815, asking him to concede some favors that might attract pardos, suggesting at least the possibility offered by the suspended constitution of 1812. The point of departure of his discussion was that "Venezuela has returned to the domination of the King thanks to the efforts of the inhabitants themselves and the armies under the Royal banner were composed almost entirely of Pardos and people belonging to the other castes." How could they be compensated? For slaves, manumission was the obvious compensation, but how about the pardos? Ceballos referred to his own experience of the past campaigns, in which "the darkest Pardo became accustomed to giving orders to whites and to treating them on at least equal terms." He concluded that ". . . in the case of these people no other means remains than to take them legally from their inferior class." But Ferdinand VII, sublimely stubborn and stupid as always, did not heed sound advice.[39]

Colored people finally had no choice but to join the patriot cause. The situation could not be better illustrated than by the dialogue that Pedro Molina of Guatemala wrote for the periodical *El genio de la Libertad* in 1821. When discussing the passionate subject of emancipation with loyalist Don Gómez, Pedro Mulato says that he has seen "Negro slaves who were very much esteemed and generously treated by their masters flee to the forest to live naked only in order to be free." Don Gómez interrupts: "These are savages, but we who descend from Spaniards and Christians. . . ." Pedro Mulato: "We should be free for that very reason. Is it my fault that I am a Mulatto so that Spaniards, the compatriots of my father but not of my mother, do not want me to become anything at all?" Don Gómez: "This is because the mixture of white and black breeds bad blood." Pedro Mulato has the last word: "In that case I would find myself ill, my friend." [40]

The promise of manumission also helped to swell the ranks of patriot armies and the fighting qualities of the former slaves won general recognition. General San Martín confessed that "the best soldier we have is the Negro and Mulatto," whereas the whites "are only fit for

[39] King (1953a), 536–537.
[40] Molina (1954), III, 771.

the cavalry." [41] Bolívar promised freedom to any slave who took up arms against the loyalists and tried to fulfill his promise to President Pétion of Haiti to abolish slavery as such. It was not his fault that abolition only got started during his time. His abolitionist attitude undoubtedly was sincere, based as it was on humanitarian considerations but also on political and military convenience.[42] But Simón Bolívar, at the same time, is a fascinating example of the criollo elite's ambivalent attitude toward the race issue.

Bolívar and the Race Issue

A draft of Bolívar's from 1815 stresses the relative harmony of racial relations in Spanish America, denying that the "difference of castes" forms any obstacle to independence. In this draft he even tried to explain away the secret of Boves' success by stating that slaves and mulattoes had been forced to attack the patriots.[43] The division that mattered for the Liberator was, of course, that between American-born and peninsulars. In his famed Letter of Jamaica from the same year, written under the shadow of the Black Legend, with explicit reference to Father Las Casas, Bolívar displayed a romantically pro-Indian attitude. Interestingly, he took the historical fact of the mestizaje as the point of departure for the political and constitutional theorizing that fills most of the document: ". . . we are . . . neither Indian nor European, but a species midway between the legitimate proprietors of this country and the Spanish usurpers. . . ." [44] In his famous message to the Congress of Angostura, Bolívar pursues the same theme:

> We must bear in mind that our people are neither European nor North American; they are a mixture of Africa and America rather than an emanation of Europe. Even Spain herself has ceased to be European because of her African blood, her institutions, and her character. It is impossible to determine with any degree of accuracy to which human family we belong. The greater portion of the native Indians has been annihilated. Europeans have mixed with Americans and Africans, and Africans with Indians and Europeans. While we have all been born of the same mother, our fathers, different in origin and in blood, are

[41] Masini (1962), 18.
[42] Griffin (1962), 59–61; Bierck (1953), 365–385. In Antioquia, Colombia, abolition was decreed as early as 1814. Zulueta (1916), 32–37.
[43] Lecuna, *Cartas*, I, 211–216.
[44] *Ibid.*, I, 190.

foreigners, and all differ visibly as to the color of their skin, a dissimilarity which places upon us an obligation of the greatest importance.

He concluded that politically the Democratic Republic offered the only solution because "legal equality is indispensable when there is physical inequality to correct, to some extent the injustice of Nature." [45]

The documents of Bolívar to which I have hitherto referred are all of a public character, and the Jamaica letters are obviously propagandistic. There is, nevertheless, no reason to doubt the sincerity of the Liberator's belief that the historical fact of miscegenation formed the very basis for the Spanish American peoples' national existence. But the race question for him was even more serious and profound. He had been raised in the aristocratic environment of the slave plantation. Since he was a delicate child and early became an orphan, it would be natural if he retained special affection for the obligatory Negro nanny. From Peru he writes to his sister María Antonia in 1825:

> I enclose a letter from my "mother" Hipólita so that you give her all she wants and do for her as if she really were my mother, because her milk has nurtured my life and I have also had no other father than she.[46]

But Bolívar had also inherited the fears and the guilt complex of the slavocrat proprietor class. There was also, it seems, some uncertainty as to his own lineage. Whether or not a great-grandmother of his was a mulatto is, of course, a trivial detail. But the very uncertainty in this matter may have profoundly concerned Bolívar himself.[47] Toward the end of his life, when admittedly his whole attitude became increasingly somber and pessimistic, he included in some of his letters passages that disclose both fears and guilt with regard to colored people. A letter to General Santander in 1826 is especially revealing. Informed about the insubordination of General Páez, the Liberator found himself in anguish:

> We are very far from the wonderful times of Athens and Rome, and we must not compare ourselves in any way to anything European. The

[45] Bolívar (1950), II, 682.
[46] Lecuna, *Cartas*, V, 19.
[47] See, e.g., Madariaga (1952), 16–17, 658–659. Lecuna (1956), I, 6–9, categorically denies any Negro or Indian ascendency but admits that the great-grandmother in question was illegitimate.

origins of our existence are most impure. All that has preceded us is enveloped in the black cloak of crime. We are the abominable off-spring of those raging beasts that came to America to waste her blood and to breed with their victims before sacrificing them. Later the fruits of these unions commingled with slaves uprooted from Africa. With such physical mixtures and such elements of morale, can we possibly place laws above heroes and principles above men? [48]

In these naked words, Simón Bolívar expresses the "tragic sense of life" of which Unamuno speaks, intimately related to the idea of criminal rape as the origin of existence and awareness of the eternal stigma of slavery.[49] At the same time, he remains the aristocrat who regards the masses with contempt mixed with fear. His concept of men of more or less dark skin, like Piar, Padilla, and even Páez shows mixed disdain and envy, because he feels that they embody the real spirit of America. By virtue of their origin, they will be the victors of tomorrow. Referring to Padilla, Bolívar writes to Santander: ". . . legal equality is not enough to satisfy the spirit of the people who want absolute equality, both in the public and the domestic sphere. Later, they will request 'Pardocracy' which is their natural and only inclination before exterminating the privileged class. . . ." In shocking contrast to his optimistic declaration of 1815, Bolívar now speaks of the "natural enmity of the colors," prophesying gloomily about the day "when the people of color will rise and put an end to everything." In a way reminiscent of Spengler, Bolívar admits the impotency of his own class and "race." Referring to Padilla and Páez, he exclaims: "These two men have the elements of power in their blood, because my [blood] is of no value in the eyes of the people." [50] There can be no doubt that the "Götterdämmerung," the last battle that loomed before the eyes of the declining and dying Bolívar, had a strong flavor of racial conflict.[51]

[48] Lecuna, *Cartas*, VI, 11.

[49] Interesting to compare this with the reflections of the modern Mexican author Octavio Paz in his *The Labyrinth of Solitude*.

[50] Lecuna, *Cartas*, IV, 307; VII, 257. He also uses the word *pardocracia* in a letter to Santander in 1825 (*ibid.*, V, 12). His sister had informed him that "Caracas is uninhabitable because of the attempts and menaces of the pardocracia."

[51] Around 1823, rumors were widespread in Gran Colombia that "Haiti, like Spain, was attempting to foment race conflict and had even stationed some 300 secret agents in Venezuela for that very purpose. . . ." Bushnell (1954), 172.

But the great battle between the races never took place. In the long wars for independence, many individuals of more or less dark skin were able to climb the social ladder because of their military merits, such as Andrés de Santa Cruz, José Antonio Páez, Vicente Guerrero, and Agustín Gamarra.[52] But, instead of replacing the traditional criollo elite, they were assimilated into it, abandoning any intention they might have had to represent the interests of the socioethnic group from which they sprang. Furthermore, for all the contrast between the lighter skin of the upper strata and the darker skin of most of those below, the new Society of Classes did not offer the rigid and well-defined borders that directly provoked attack. There were always some of darker skin who, thanks to military or professional merit, or by sheer astuteness, participated in the upward mobility, whereas, now and then, "whites" were sinking to the bottom of the social structure.[53] It is true that, by the middle of the nineteenth century, intellectuals and professionals of the middle strata, conspicuous among them the mestizos, began to form a most influential part of the liberal parties, especially in Mexico under the *Reforma* (the period of turmoil and profound political change, 1854–1876). But their attack against the elite (still mostly criollo) was not ethnically dictated. The oligarchy was attacked for being an oligarchy, not for being composed of criollos.

The rebellions of the indígenas, which had been frequent under the Spanish regime, continued during most of the national era. Among the leaders, not a few mestizos can be found by the mid-nineteenth century, such as José María Barrera in the so-called Caste War among the Maya Indians of Yucatán.[54] But such mestizos had identified themselves with the Indians.

Apart, perhaps, from the Dominican Republic with its border problem with Negro Haiti, in Spanish America only Venezuela seems to have experienced any major "racial" influence on its political life. If we can trust the testimony left by some contemporary observers, the Monagas brothers' regime demagogically fomented the hatred of the masses for the more white-looking elite. These tensions culminated in the sanguinary so-called Federal War of 1859–1863.[55] This horrid

[52] Presidents of Bolivia-Peru, Venezuela, Mexico, and Peru, respectively.
[53] A good example of social advancement is the mulatto José Romero portrayed by Feliú Cruz (1942), 183–225.
[54] Reed (1964); Armillas (1962), 166–168.
[55] Gilmore (1964), 40–41; Hudson (1964), 236–239.

civil war, excellently described by novelist Rómulo Gallegos in his *Poor Negro*, succeeded in bringing about extensive socioracial leveling, a great achievement that contrasts strikingly with the utter sterility of its political consequences. From that time onward, Venezuela, for all its political instability and lack of equilibrium, was able to achieve more harmonious (or less disharmonious) relations between the ethnic elements than almost any other Spanish American country.

In Brazil, some of the rebellions and uprisings in the northeast during the imperial regency seem to have had a socioracial content. Carlos Rama says that "with a basis of peasants, these [rebellions] blindly, often brutally, but dominated by the presence of proletarians, aimed at destroying the system of exploitation on which the society of castes rested in Brazil." [56] In the northeast backlands, anarchist and messianic movements succeeded one another, among them the rebellion of Canudos in the 1890's, immortalized by Euclides da Cunha. Less consciously than the rebels of the coast undoubtedly, the backlands fanatics expressed the frustration and resentment felt by the oppressed strata of the Brazilian people.

If we were to try to summarize the facts presented in this chapter, we should make it clear that the built-in tensions of the Society of Castes really threatened to produce a civil struggle along socioethnic lines. But the criollo elite understood how to preserve its control, with the peninsulars attracting much of the accumulated hatred. The legal framework defining the Society of Castes was abolished. Nevertheless, the stratification into classes preserved most of the traditional distance between the basic ethnic groups, even though, on an individual level, social mobility, upward as well as downward, now and then affected persons of different colors. Naturally enough, socioracial prejudice did not disappear, but its expression became more subtle. Therefore it was less easily exposed than that of colonial society.[57]

[56] Rama (1957), 344. See also Carneiro (1964), 31–32.

[57] In faraway corners more traditional attitudes may have prevailed. In Santa Cruz de la Sierra in Bolivia, the French traveler Castelnau noticed in 1845 the "vanity of caste" of the ladies who treated all servants who had "some drop of mixed blood . . . as Cholas, even if at times they are whiter than their mistresses." Quoted by Vázquez-Machicado (1956), 183.

VII

Social Change in the Countryside

Indian Population Decline and
Forced Labor Systems

In order to understand how the Spaniard-Indian dichotomy was gradually being replaced by that of *hacendados* and *peones* we must consider rural evolution in Spanish America.[1] Until very recent times the majority by far of the population of what we call Latin America lived in the countryside, making a precarious livelihood by farming. Despite this preponderance, the agrarian history of Latin America has received only scanty treatment. Like most historians, students of Latin America's past have usually been town dwellers themselves, unfamiliar with, and little interested in, rural conditions. Neither does the agrarian history of Latin America fit into a chronological framework determined by the political division between the colonial and national periods. The research that has been carried out by François Chevalier, Charles Gibson, Orlando Fals Borda, Mario Góngora, and a few others covers only limited regions and periods.[2] It is most uncertain how valid generalizations made on this basis will be. Thus, even an account as brief as the present one has to be largely hypothetical.

[1] In this chapter I have chosen to omit Brazil. The plantation zone will be dealt with in Chapter VIII.
[2] Chevalier (1956); Fals Borda (1957); Góngora (1960).

91

Our point of departure is the decline of the Indian population after contact with Europeans. This decline accelerated during the latter part of the sixteenth century. In New Spain, the epidemics of matlalzáhuatl of 1576–1579 were crucial. The epidemic of 1585–1591 in Peru seems to have been similarly important.[3] It was the drastic decline in Indian population, the main source of labor, that was chiefly responsible for what Woodrow Borah has called the "Century of Depression," when both food production and the production of the mines suffered from lack of manpower. The large estate, the *hacienda*, grew out of the new and harsh economic climate, just as the large estates were formed in the early Middle Ages in Europe. The haciendas, more or less self-sufficient, usually had a surplus to sell. Despite its (more often than not) extralegal origin, the hacienda was a normal feature in Spanish American rural society toward the end of the seventeenth century.[4] The motives behind the foundation of the haciendas were not only economic. The hacendados, most of them merchants, miners, and cattle barons, wanted power and prestige. Although there were some encomenderos among them, Silvio Zavala has shown that there was no direct connection between encomienda and hacienda. The concession of an encomienda did not imply any right to the lands of the Indians.[5]

By the mid-sixteenth century, the encomienda had lost its character as a labor system in most of Spanish America. According to royal regulations, the Indians were to pay their tribute to encomenderos in commodities or cash, and not in labor as before. Little by little, these regulations came to be enforced. Consequently, labor needed in agriculture could not be obtained via the encomienda system. When the encomienda Indians no longer had to perform labor for their encomenderos, new systems of forced, but paid, labor were established. Known as *repartimiento* or *cuatequil* in New Spain and *mita* in Peru,[6] these systems, provided that a fixed proportion of the Indians would be sent out to work for a certain number of weeks in rotation during the year. A functionary called the *juez repartidor* saw to it that all who needed Indian labor got their share: those in charge of public works,

---

[3] Borah (1951); Dobyns (1963).

[4] On the hacienda, Chevalier (1956); Wolf (1962), 201ff.; Vázquez (1961), 12–17.

[5] Zavala (1940, 1948). Góngora, on his part, introduces the following modification: ". . . factual, not legal relation. . . ." Borde and Góngora (1956), I, 29.

[6] Haring (1963), 58–62.

the mine owners, and the hacendados.[7] It was difficult to obtain enough workers for the hacendados, who found the frequent changes in the labor force under this system another unwelcome feature. The supply of farm hands under the repartimiento system seems to have been discontinued in the central parts of Mexico and Peru before the middle of the seventeenth century. In central Colombia, we are told, the rural repartimiento disappeared around 1740.[8] Having no more forced Indian labor, how should the hacendados resolve their labor problem? Might Negro slaves provide the solution? Negroes were sometimes used as servants, cowherds, or artisans within the hacienda economy, but they were far too expensive to be used on a large scale in haciendas other than really remunerative sugar plantations and the like. Therefore, voluntary Indian labor was the only resource that remained. From the latter part of the sixteenth century onward, the authorities, both civil and ecclesiastic, had devoted much energy to gathering the Indians into landholding villages or towns all over Spanish America. These reducciones soon housed most of the Indian population. Though they had lost their status as missions, these settlements were supposed to remain *pueblos de indios*, or Indian communities, as differentiated from the villages or towns of the "Spaniards" (non-Indians).

Indian Free Labor and Peonage

After the early seventeenth century, we notice that more and more Indians from the pueblos de indios voluntarily offered to work for the landowners in exchange for wages fixed by contract. The relationship of this growth to the decline of the repartimiento system in regard to farm labor is obvious. These Indians, called *gañanes*, usually continued to reside in their villages for a long time. They retained their legal status as Indians and were subject to the jurisdiction of their own municipal officers. They were liable to tribute.[9] In fact, their main reason for seeking jobs on a hacienda often may have been to obtain the money required to pay their tribute. At least in New Spain in the early seventeenth century, the patrons were put in charge of collecting

[7] Gibson (1954), 593–594; *HSAI*, II, 371–377.
[8] Ospina Pérez (1955), 14–16.
[9] They even had to perform cuatequil. Gibson (1964), 247. See also Góngora (1960), 31.

the tributes of their gañanes, beginning the separation of the Indian from his native community.

The Indian town governments vainly tried to resist the flow of tribute payers to the haciendas.[10] For the hacendados, the *gañán* really solved the problem of how to obtain permanent labor when manpower was becoming more and more scarce. The eagerness with which the hacendados sought to expand their domains at the expense of the Indian communities is partly explained by their need for Indian labor. According to Chevalier, the best means of obtaining gañanes was to deprive the Indian villages of their lands.[11] Until the middle of the eighteenth century many gañanes continued to live in the Indian communities. A geographical account of New Spain from these years mentions that a village in the district of Tepeaca "is settled by fifty-five families of Indians who work as gañanes on the haciendas in the neighborhood." Taking the point of view of the hacienda, the same account mentions that around Tenancingo there were six haciendas where about fifty families of Spaniards and mestizos lived. They were the foremen; most of the farm hands were the Indian gañanes of Tenancingo.[12] But gradually this situation changed. More and more gañanes left their communities for good to settle on the hacienda lands, partly because the hacendados offered them a plot of land to cultivate or grazing grounds for their animals. Also, they did so simply because life in the communities was becoming more and more difficult. When the population of the communities decreased, the onerous municipal charges had to be divided among fewer individuals and, since the tribute often was collected according to outmoded tax rolls, this obligation became increasingly burdensome. As we shall see, there was also a greater and greater influx of mestizos and other strangers, who often disturbed and dealt harshly with the Indians. Such conditions made, or seemed to make the hacienda, like the medieval manor, a refuge and guarantee of personal security.

At the same time, the act of moving to a hacienda, particularly if it was not the nearest one, might also enable the Indian to escape from his legal status. "They live at their own will and turn themselves into Mestizos and other kinds of people," as a contemporary document

[10] Borah (1951), 41; Gibson (1954), 595.
[11] Chevalier (1956), 170.
[12] Villa-Señor y Sánchez (1748), II, 203, 255.

from Chile puts it.[13] Vagabond Indians seem to have become very numerous during the late colonial period. A tribute assessment from New Spain in 1806 indicates that in the province of Guanajuato no fewer than 164,879 Indians were classified as "laboríos [migrant Indian workers] and vagrants," whereas only 74,852 were still living in their own communities. This may have been a somewhat regional exception, but, even so, it is well documented that a great many Indians were moving around and seeking jobs in other regions as well.[14] Undoubtedly, most of these Indians on the move sooner or later were absorbed by the haciendas to serve as gañanes or peones. The classic device of tying the worker to the property consisted of giving him credits that he was unable to pay back, placing him in debt slavery or, rather, debt serfdom. As early as 1567, a royal decree prohibited this kind of abuse. But, on the whole, the Crown and the authorities did little to prevent this device from being expanded and institutionalized.[15] In 1784, the viceroy of New Spain even issued regulations governing peonage. According to these regulations, new workers were not to be accepted on a hacienda unless they could show that they were free from debt in other haciendas, but the new employer might promise to pay their previous debts.[16] In that way a class of practically hereditary rural workers was formed. But the mechanism of indebtedness only partially explains this important phenomenon. Recent research on the valley of Mexico has made it clear that there the peones' indebtedness was of little import.[17] A scholar familiar with central Colombia says the same about that region.[18] At least for the colonial period, the essential fact was that, in spite of everything, life as a peon on a hacienda was the best alternative available to the Indians of Spanish America.

The process that I have just briefly outlined differed greatly in other parts of Spanish America. In Chile the encomienda, also in the form of labor paid as tribute to the encomendero, persisted much longer than

[13] Quoted by Carmagnani (1963), 24.
[14] Wolf (1957), 190–191. See also Gibson (1964), 149–150; Martin (1957); López Sarrelangue (1962), 520.
[15] Borah (1951), 37–41.
[16] See Zavala (1944), 729–744, on the efforts of the viceroys of New Spain to regulate peonage between 1589 and 1786. A revealing document from 1702 is in Zavala and Casteló (1946), 149–150.
[17] Gibson (1964), 249–255.
[18] Ospina Pérez (1955), 18.

in most other parts. Even Indian slavery (e.g., among the hostile Arau-canos) existed in Chile until the end of the seventeenth century, when the ex-slaves were left in the keeping of their former masters. This transitional form was abolished as late as 1703. A careful study on a small district not far from Santiago, the valley of Puangue, shows a surprising variety of categories of farm labor. Labor from the encomi-endas and the Indian villages both supplied the encomenderos with labor and benefited other landowners as well. The Indians were either hired out or simply loaned to them by the encomenderos, or contracts were concluded with the Indians in accordance with existing tariffs. Other small groups of Indians settled on the haciendas, such as Arau-canian captives, Yanaconas, and Indian refugees. Sometimes these In-dians were grouped into new encomiendas, sometimes they became outright slaves or peones.[19]

The "Regulations of Wages to be Paid to the Indians" issued by the viceroy in 1687 provide us with interesting facts about the cate-gories of labor in Peru. The Indians attached to haciendas (*Indios agregados a las haciendas*) were to receive the same wages, 3 *reales* per day, as the Indians performing mita (*Indios mitayos*). Although the former also received plots to cultivate, the viceroy thought that the landowners benefited enough by having these Indians and their sons continuously available that the comparatively high wages were justified. In southeastern Peru the indios agregados were called *arrenderos* (ten-ants), whereas on the coast the old word "yanacona" was used. The regulations forbade the use of Indians as domestic servants (*indios pongos*) and the distribution of Indian workers to the hacendados by the corregidores and caciques (*indios picotas*).[20] There is, of course, no reason to believe that this prohibition was enforced.

In what is now Ecuador, rural mita was widespread and persistent. Many mitayos stayed on the haciendas for good. A critical observer, Antonio de Ulloa, a young naval officer who visited the country in the 1730's, states that the mitayos received wages of about 14 to 18 pesos a year from the hacendados in addition to a small plot of land to cultivate. For this they had to work 300 days a year except holidays. After 8 pesos for tribute was deducted, the Indian had not enough left to support his family and to meet his obligations to the parish

[19] Borde and Góngora (1956), I, 72–73.
[20] The document constitutes MS. 1426, B. Mendel Collection, University of Indiana, Bloomington, Ind.

priest, for example. Thus, he usually had to ask the hacendado to advance him some corn. The latter did so, but at an outrageous price.[21]

In New Granada, where the rural mita also persisted until the mid-eighteenth century, there seems to have been a direct link between this form of labor and the permanent peones of the haciendas.[22] In Guatemala, the repartimiento system seems to have continued as the principal supply of labor for the hacendados. Under the name *mandamiento* it experienced a revival during the latter part of the nineteenth century.[23]

In Yucatán, the encomiendas proved even more tenacious than they were in Chile. It was not until the end of the eighteenth century that they began to disappear. The haciendas obtained their labor mainly in two ways. There were indebted resident peones (*peones acasillados*), often mestizos, and wage earners who came from the neighboring Maya villages, the so-called *luneros* (derived from *lunes*, Monday, their usual day of work). The Maya villages were sometimes within, sometimes outside the haciendas, but usually depended on them for their water supply, critical in this dry region.[24]

Once settled on a hacienda as a peon, the Indian had to mingle with people belonging to other ethnic groups in his new environment. If there was no miscegenation, at least there was acculturation. He necessarily adopted the Spanish language. Woodrow Borah therefore states that "Debt peonage, ironically, helped to forge the Mexican nation." [25] This observation could be extended to other parts of Spanish America.

Mestizo Penetration into Indian Villages

But the transformation and, to a certain extent, the mestization of the rural sector of Spanish America came about not only because the Indians settled down in the "Spanish" environment of the hacienda, but also because the mestizos settled in the Indian communities. It was a double process.

Although it is difficult to prove and measure because of the vague terminology and deficiencies in the quantitative source material, there was clearly a rapid increase in the racially mixed population during

21 Juan and Ulloa (1953), 209–211; Pérez (1947), 120.
22 Fals Borda (1957), 78–80.
23 Zavala (1945), 81–85.
24 Strickom (1965), 45–46.
25 Borah (1951), 42. Cf. Carmagnani (1963), 28–29.

the colonial period. The "so-called Whites" (including European immigrants, criollos, and mestizos) in New Spain increased (according to Borah's figures, to which we have added for comparison his figures for the Indians) as follows:

Year	"Whites" in New Spain	in Central Mexico	Indians Central Mexico
1570	63,000	57,000	4,409,000 (1565)
1646	125,000	114,000	1,500,000 (1650)
1742	565,000	465,000	1,500,000
1772	784,000	586,000	
1793	1,050,000	780,000	3,700,000 [26]

Even Angel Rosenblat's extremely cautious calculations show a relative increase for the "castas" (mixed-bloods) from a few per cent in 1650 to about 25 per cent in 1825 for the whole of Spanish America. But I think he greatly underrates the figures for the castas.[27] The increase in the mestizo population is especially striking from the mid-seventeenth century onward.[28] It is likely that most of these mestizos were born and raised in the principal "Spanish" towns, in the mining districts, and in the regional and local administrative centers (*cabeceras*) that had originally been pueblos de indios. On the other hand, available sources suggest that very often the children begotten by Spanish and mestizo vagrants stayed with their Indian mothers and were assimilated into the maternal group. We do not know whether these individuals were listed as Indians in the tax rolls or if they were able to avoid paying tribute by referring to their status as "mestizo," though otherwise completely Indianized.[29] Vagrants, sometimes transformed into wage earners or peddlers, were not the only non-Indians who visited the Indian communities.[30] There were also foremen and representatives of the encomenderos, mestizo artisans, and collectors of tithes and other taxes. Toward the end of the seventeenth century there was hardly any room for the increased mestizo population in the "Spanish" cities and towns. On the other hand, after the dynamic sixteenth century, only a few new urban centers were established before

[26] Borah (1951), 18.

[27] Rosenblat (1954), I, 36, 59. Cf. Carmagnani (1963), 28–29.

[28] See, e.g., the figures on militiamen in Góngora (1960), 59–66.

[29] According to Gibson (1964), 144, 147, "One may suspect that the Spaniards usually classified Mestizos as Indians in order to render them liable to tribute payment and other kinds of obligation. . . ." What I have seen of the records leaves me with the impression, however, that even Indianized mestizos resisted such pretensions, probably most often successfully.

[30] In Peru the vagrants went under the name of "soldiers."

the eighteenth century. At the same time, the Indian towns and villages were more and more depopulated, not only by epidemics but also by desertion to the haciendas, as pointed out above. The vacuum was filled by the mestizos. An Indianophile contemporary, a parish priest from the country now called Ecuador, observed in 1695 that the primary reason for the mestizo infiltration into the Indian villages was to exploit their labor. Here everybody, he says, considers himself a master and gentleman, everybody from "the Spaniard to the most miserable Mestizo or Indian who dresses himself in such a way as to escape from tribute. . . . They join the Indians and settle down in their villages in order to have them available day and night for any purpose. . . ." [31] I believe, however, that the mestizos were attracted above all by the land that the Indians, diminishing in numbers as they were, no longer cultivated. By the late seventeenth or early eighteenth century it was no longer easy for a mestizo or even a poor Spaniard to satisfy his hunger for land to cultivate, for most of the arable areas had been divided among the large haciendas and the Indian communities. He would in any case probably have to cultivate the land as a tenant, not as an owner. Often, the Indian communities were interested in having the mestizos rent at least part of their lands, because they needed cash in order to pay their tribute. Sometimes the communities also sold land to the newcomers, though legislation strictly prohibited such sale. A royal decree of 1646, which repeated the old prohibition against non-Indians settling among the natives, characteristically added: ". . . even if they have bought land in the Indian villages." [32] Notwithstanding the prohibitions, we find more and more mestizos living in the villages of the Indians or nearby in modest ranchos. The governor of Soconuzco in northwestern Central America reported in 1673 that most of the numerous Spaniards, Negroes, mulattoes, and mestizos in the district ("in most cases reputed to be Spaniards") lived among the Indians in their villages. A smaller part were scattered around the Indian villages. [33] It is difficult to get a clear idea of the new structure of the rural population in the seventeenth century, since most sources provide figures only for Indians paying tribute. But there are exceptions. We know that in the 1680's no fewer than 300 mestizos (*vecinos ladinos*) lived in the twenty-five pueblos de indios of the Zapotitlán province of northern Central America. Their presence must have been

[31] Pérez de Tudela Bueso (1960), 331.
[32] *RI*, VI–III–22.
[33] Mörner (1964b), 145.

tacitly approved by the authorities, for they were supposed to recruit four companies of militia.[34] From the mid-eighteenth century onward, the sources showing the population pattern in the countryside are much more abundant. The authors of important geographical accounts, such as José Antonio de Villa-Señor of New Spain, Bishop Pedro Cortés y Larraz of Guatemala, and Basilio Vicente de Oviedo of New Granada no longer try to hide the fact that the so-called pueblos de indios often had a numerous non-Indian population as well. On reading these sources, we are left with the impression that around the middle of the eighteenth century there were one or two "Spanish" families in almost every pueblo de indios and that in the larger ones often a third or half the inhabitants were non-Indians.[35] Apart from regional differences, it is obvious that the larger Indian agglomerations (cabeceras) were more heavily infiltrated than the smaller ones (*sujetos*). In spite of all the non-Indians present, the Indian communities continued to be governed by their own municipalities, and the mestizos were legally excluded from membership in these.[36] It is no wonder that there was often tension between the two groups. But sometimes, it seems, the relations were comparatively harmonious. When the grievances voiced in the legal documentation by the Indians against some mestizo were very minor, it may be concluded that the situation, after all, was not too bad. Certainly, the eighteenth century witnessed increased miscegenation in the Indian villages. An inspection tour by a high administrator in central New Granada in 1755–1756 revealed that the so-called pueblos de indios in the district had a population of no more than 28,000 Indians, compared with 59,000 non-Indians, mostly mestizos (vecinos).[37] When the Indians of a pueblo de indios had melted to a small minority, the transformation of the place into a "Spanish town" was relatively easy. It sometimes happened, too, that the authorities transferred an Indian minority to another pueblo de indios, where they came to form an unwelcome additional group (*agregados*). At the same time, their old lands were divided among the Spaniards and mestizos who had remained in their former village when they were ousted. This was the application in reverse of the obso-

[34] *Ibid.*, 149.

[35] Villa-Señor y Sanchez (1748); Cortés y Larraz (1958); Oviedo (1930).

[36] Góngora (1960), 80–81, refers to a surprising decision made by the audiencia of Chile in 1748, according to which vagrants married to Indians (but not single vagrants) should be allowed to stay in the villages if they contributed toward paying the tribute of the Indians.

[37] Mörner (1963), 74–76.

lete laws imposing residential separation between Indians and non-Indians that were once enacted in order to protect the natives against intruders! But many mestizo farmers (owners or tenants) cultivating the soil of the Indian villages, continued an extralegal existence until emancipation. Only then were they confirmed in their property rights and their presence among the Indians was legally sanctioned.

"Mestizo" and "Indian" Become Social Concepts

The demographic surplus of mestizos was not channeled toward the pueblos de indios alone. There was another flow toward the haciendas. There had always been mestizos who served as foremen and in other positions of trust. But it is interesting to notice the steady increase in the number of mestizo tenants. In New Spain we find the *rancheros* renting outlying portions of the haciendas in exchange for services rendered to the hacendados.[38] In New Granada there were both Spanish and mestizo tenants, some very poor, others relatively well off.[39] The only study of any depth referring to this social category seems to be that made by Mario Góngora on central Chile. According to the traditional view, the *inquilino*, the characteristic rural proletarian of Chile, derived from a category of Indian workers of the post-encomienda period. But Góngora convincingly shows that, instead, the inquilino developed from a form of non-Indian tenancy. Within the pastoral economy of seventeenth-century Chile, the landowners let out land to other Spaniards and mestizos as *préstamos de tierras* (loans of land), in exchange for an almost symbolic rent and some easily performed services. But, during the eighteenth century, the number of tenants increased at the same time as the growing wheat export to Peru caused a remarkable rise in land values. Thus, as we would expect, the rents were increased considerably. Toward the end of the century many tenants found themselves obliged to pay their rent by day labor, which lowered their social status. Now they were called inquilinos, and their pieces of land grew smaller. But, as Góngora sees it, their real transformation into a miserable proletariat took place during the nineteenth century, a process mainly to be explained by their increasing numbers.[40]

This agrarian phenomenon may be compared with an interesting parallel phenomenon that has been studied in the mining district of

[38] Chevalier (1956), 226.
[39] Fals Borda (1957), 84.
[40] Góngora (1960), *passim*.

Norte Chico in the northern part of central Chile. Employers were able to attract workers by offering them "loans of veins" to exploit on their own account. Later, thanks to the debt device, they were able to restrict the movements of these workers. This device, which, as we have seen, was often used with the Indians on the haciendas, in the mines, and in the workshops, was found equally expedient for people of Spanish or mixed origin. The study of Norte Chico labor indicates that 49 per cent of the mine workers from 1720 to 1750 were "whites," 21 per cent "mestizos," and 30 per cent "Indians." For the years 1750–1800, the author states that no less than 79 per cent were classified as "whites," 14 per cent as "mestizos," and only 7 per cent as "Indians." [41] A similar breakdown of hacienda labor probably would have shown a similar trend. It is rather obvious that the criterion of ethnic classification had become more generous both for mestizos who wanted to pass as "whites" and for Indians who wanted to pass as "mestizos."

On the eve of emancipation, the designation "Indian" had already, in the rural sector, became mainly a social instead of a racial concept. The "Indian" was generally a member of an Indian community that functioned in accordance with the Hispano-Indian norms set down in the Laws of the Indies. He was a full-fledged member of that community, as distinguished from the Spanish or mestizo vecinos, who lived among the Indians but did not share their legal status.

If he left his native community and his district for good, the way was open for the enterprising Indian to change his status. In the central parts of the South American Andes, the vague and transitory name *cholo* helped to bridge the gap between "Indian" and "mestizo"; that is, between community peasant and the mestizo farmers and artisans.[42] When the legislators and administrators of the era of emancipation introduced the new word "indígena," this step reflected their awareness that the division between the rural groups had become social rather than racial. It was also an attempt to remove the disdain attached to the designation "Indian." Near the end of the nineteenth century, similar efforts, with the same basic motivation, were made by replacing "indígena" with "poor peasant" (*labrador pobre, campesino*).[43]

[41] Carmagnani (1963), 52–64.
[42] Kubler (1952), 36–37.
[43] See, e.g., *Métodos* (1954), 118–119. The president of Guatemala in 1876 decreed that the indígenas of San Pedro de Sacatepéquez who from 1877 onwards used ladino dress would "for legal purposes be declared to be ladinos"! Skinner-Klée (1954), 33, 117–118.

The "Indian" Policy of the
National Governments

The first national governments eagerly tried to equalize the two
large groups into which the rural population was divided. At least, this
is the impression conveyed by the rhetorical heat of the constitutional
and political debate. Bolívar abolished the Indian tribute in Gran Colombia in 1821. General San Martín did the same in the patriot-held
territory in Peru in the same year. But as early as 1826, the tribute
was reintroduced in Peru under another name: *contribución de indígenas*. Two years later the same thing happened in Colombia. It was
argued that fiscal equality, which had been introduced to benefit the
Indians, far from doing so had actually made their situation even
worse, and that the Indians themselves had asked for some kind of
single tax.[44] Theoretically, the contribución de indígenas, at least in
Peru, had a counterpart in the *contribución de castas*, but the source
materials indicate that by and large only the Indians were actually paying their tax. In 1854, when the Peruvian treasury was being filled,
thanks to the revenues flowing from the exporting of guano, President
Castilla finally abolished the contribución de indígenas. He admitted
that it had been a principal reason why "Independence, achieved by so
many sacrifices, remains an empty word for the majority of the Peruvian people who live in the most severe slavery and the most complete
debasement." [45]

Even more important than the taxation question was that of the
collective ownership of land by the Indian communities. This phenomenon did not conform to the tenets of economic liberalism. In
Gran Colombia, a law passed in 1821 determined that the lands of the
Indian communities, the *resguardos de indígenas*, were to be divided
among the Indians as private holdings within five years. The legislation
was applied during the 1830's, though under the condition that the
new holdings would remain inalienable for another ten years. In this
way most of the resguardos in central Colombia disappeared, though
some have managed to survive.[46] In 1958, I visited a little town not far
from Bogotá, which, from the administrative point of view, remained

[44] Rubio Orbe (1954), 20. The Spanish regime abolished the tribute as
early as 1811. Kubler (1952), 3.
[45] LIP (1948), 34–36.
[46] Fals Borda (1957), 98–100. See also Friede (1944).

103

divided between an ordinary municipality and a resguardo de indígenas. The members of the two groups belonged to the same physical and cultural mestizo type; family tradition determined to which group one belonged. In Peru, Bolívar decreed in 1824 that the lands of the communities should be divided. At first the new Indian landlords were forbidden to sell their land prior to the year 1850, but this precautionary measure was soon repealed. The door was then opened for ruthless whites and mestizos to deprive the inexperienced Indian landowners of their land. Nevertheless, quite a number of communities managed to survive without the protection of legislation or the authorities. The same was true in Bolivia.[47]

In Mexico the agrarian policies administered by the various state and local authorities differed considerably during the first decades of the national era. A decisive step was taken with the Lerdo Law of 1856, which decreed that all collectively held land, that of the Indian communities as well as that of the Church, was to be broken up. Though the Church lands were the main concern of the "Reforma" liberals, they also dreamed of the Indians becoming money-conscious freeholders. In a great many Mexican communities, the gradual application of the Lerdo Law spelled disaster. About 40 per cent of the communities somehow managed to survive, however, until the Revolution of 1910. As everywhere in Latin America, the Mexican liberals, in pursuing the noble ideal of legal equality among all citizens, lacked understanding of the agrarian problem. Carlos María Bustamante was one of the very few who questioned the prudence of the agrarian policy. In a debate in 1824 he exclaimed: "I think I hear people say that there are no Indians any more, that we are all Mexicans. . . . This sounds like a brave illusion to me, an illusion to remedy real and serious ills. . . . No Indians exist any more but the same needs from which the Indians suffered still exist." For all its good intentions, liberalism in power made the Indians' situation worse, even though the policy was modified somewhat in favor of the Indians toward the end of the long dictatorship of Porfirio Díaz (1876–1911).[48]

[47] Sáenz (1933), 203–206. Cf. Romero (1949), 446. A decree of 1828 recognized, without distinction, "the so-called Indians and Mestizos as possessors" of their lands. *LIP* (1948), 22.

[48] *Métodos* (1954), 122–130; González de Cossío (1958), 39–55. Bustamante quoted by Chávez Orozco (1943), 369. Referring to the Indian communities, a liberal journalist in 1856 commented: ". . . the communism is opposed to liberty and civilization" (!). Reyes Héroles (1961), III, 611.

Conservatism, the other major trend in Latin American politics during the nineteenth century, had no better record with regard to the Indians than did liberalism. The indifference of the conservatives to their fate seems to have been rather complete. The Mexican conservative leader Lucas Alamán, otherwise distinguished, is reported to have said that "it would be dangerous to enable the Indians to read the papers." [49]

Social Effects of Mid-Century Economic Change

But political ideologies formed only one side of the Indian dilemma. By the middle of the nineteenth century, the economic and technological revolution, radiating from western Europe, reached Latin America. The increased demand in the more developed countries of Europe and North America for the raw materials and foodstuffs of Latin America brought profit to some haciendas for the first time in their history. Consequently, the demand for manpower increased, as did the temptation to exploit more harshly the available labor. Increased revenues enabled many hacendados to withdraw from their estates in order to reside in the capital of the nation or, realizing their most optimistic dreams, in Paris. Under absentee ownership, labor relations on the hacienda became less paternalist and more crude. [50]

In Yucatán, the expanded sugar plantations increased demand for Maya labor. This kind of work was more difficult for the Indians to combine with the cultivation of their own plots than services on the traditional cattle estancias had been. Thus the pressure of the hacendados helped to provoke the terrible uprising of 1847, the "Caste War," which was to cost 100,000 lives. Once western Yucatán had been pacified, the henequen plantations that replaced the destroyed sugar plantations subjected the surviving Maya Indians to even worse conditions, transforming them into a miserable rural proletariat. [51]

In Guatemala, the demand of coffee plantations for Indian labor provides the backdrop to the "liberal" policy of Justo Rufino Barrios, who abolished the Indian communities in 1877. The Indians of Guatemala were distributed to the coffee producers by the local authorities to serve in rotation, from one to four weeks yearly. This "mandamiento"

[49] *Métodos* (1954), 116.
[50] Summary by Mosk (1948).
[51] Strickom (1965); Reed (1964).

105

meant that the colonial labor system was completely revived. In 1934, Guatemala introduced legislation to prevent "vagrancy," which in fact meant that Indians had to serve between 100 and 150 days yearly outside the village where they resided. This form of discriminatory exploitation was not abolished until 1945. When the United Fruit Company started cultivating bananas in Guatemala, in 1906, the demand for Indian labor increased. As distinct from the coffee plantations, banana cultivation took place on the Caribbean seashore, far from where most Indians lived. Consequently, many Indians who went to the coast lost their ties with their native communities and became mestizos (or "ladinos," the Central American term). The migrant Indian laborers in the highlands, on the other hand, usually retained these links and their Indian status.[52]

The same age that witnessed the high bourgeoisie's rise and prosperity in Latin America also witnessed deterioration in the living conditions of the working masses, most of them people of darker skin. Commercial agriculture and mining convey the same general impression. The rural masses were unable to set up any organized resistance against the ruthless exploitation. Occasional rebellions were put down efficiently and cruelly, as in Mexico under Porfirio Díaz. Ambiguously and vaguely worded legislation as well as administrative practices sanctioned various systems of labor and tenancy in Latin America, all of which favored the large landholders at the expense of labor. In exchange for letting the workers cultivate some small plot of land, the hacendados obtained very cheap labor. The natural increase of the rural proletariat helped to maintain this situation or made it still more extreme. Today, the relative increase in the marginal rural population often is higher than that of better situated strata. Probably the same imbalance existed during an earlier period as well, though statistics are unreliable or lacking.[53]

The statements above apply of course to both "Indian" and "mestizo" proletarians. Let us now look at the former. As I have pointed

[52] Dessaint (1962), 323–354, quotes a French traveler during the 1860's: "Tous les travaux des haciendas sont généralement faits par des Indiens nomades. . . ." See also Stavenhagen (1963), 70 and *passim*.

[53] *ILO* (1957), *passim*. Costales (1962), 15–36, affirms that the *huasipungo* in Equador (described in Jorge Icaza's famous novel) is derived from the rural mita, but her historical exposition is very sketchy. As late as 1954 the *huasipungueros* formed 7.5 per cent of the rural population of the Ecuadorean Sierra.

out, the process that divided the Indian population into two parts, permanent peons and community peasants, and sometimes also part-time wage earners, resulted mainly from conditions prevalent during the eighteenth century. As a consequence of emancipation, the communities' legal foundations were undermined or disappeared altogether. On the other hand, existing forms of labor and tenancy received legal sanction. When, during the nineteenth century, the rural masses came to be more harshly exploited, the exploitation of the Indians took other, peculiar forms, the mandamiento in Guatemala, for example. In the South American Andes the *pongueaje*, or certain domestic services apart from labor to be rendered to the hacendado, became both burdensome and humiliating. Different forms of gratis work for public and ecclesiastical authorities were imposed on the Indians in particular.[54] The characteristic *fiesta* system that we meet in Indian communities, whereby yearly elected *cargueros* have to finance expensive religious celebrations, seems to be of greatest benefit to outside interests such as the suppliers. We might therefore be justified in classifying the fiesta as merely another form of exploitation of the Indians, as does Marvin Harris.[55]

In the early years of the nineteenth century there were more or less numerous Indian populations almost everywhere in Spanish America.[56] Toward the end of the century only Mexico, Guatemala, Ecuador, Peru, and Bolivia housed Indian populations of any great size. Evidently these countries also had the most numerous Indian populations at the beginning of the century. But it might be expected that the acculturation and assimilation that were so advanced late in the colonial period would have much reduced the Indian sector in the five countries during the nineteenth century. Whereas the Indians were

[54] The best survey is in *ILO* (1953), 368–385. A good illustration from 1828 is Dessaint (1962), 327–328. Called *faena*, draft labor in Peru was the continuation of the colonial mita. *HSAI*, II, 354. Vazquez (1961), 28, states that the pongueaje, despite the legal prohibition in 1821, still is "widespread in the Sierra and is not seldom found in the houses of judges, members of Congress, political and ecclesiastical functionaries and Communist leaders."

[55] Harris (1964), 25–35. See also Stavenhagen (1963), 82–84. Marshall Sucre tried in vain to suppress this kind of exploitation in Bolivia in 1826. Flores Moncayo (1953), 40–41, 57–58.

[56] The different grades of mestizaje and acculturation in the interior of Argentina in the early nineteenth century are described well by the Swedish traveler Graaner (1949), 33–34. See also *IPGH* (1961), 96. It is calculated that there were still 48,000 Indians in central Chile by 1813, in addition to those in the border region. Jara (1956), 14–15.

absorbed in the countries where they already were in the minority, acculturation and assimilation in the five countries where they formed the majority actually slowed down in the nineteenth century. When we consider the integrationist aims of Latin American liberalism, this fact is indeed paradoxical. George Kubler shows that the province of Huánuco in the Peruvian highlands had a mestizo majority in 1796 but had reverted to an Indian majority at some time before 1854. Kubler thinks that this and other retrogressions were caused by the isolation and bad economic conditions in the early national period, when many impoverished mestizos in outlying parts lost their status.[57] As for the Indian communities, the economic depression of the early national period and the civil wars probably made them more isolationist, more closed against the outer world, and more marginal.[58] When the economic situation changed in the latter half of the nineteenth century, the vitality and capitalist dynamics of the national society made the retrogression of the surviving Indian communities even more striking. The place assigned by the new society to the Indians within its economic class structure was the lowest of all. From then on, Indians who had lost their lands, formerly the key to their social identity, tended to remain Indians. In the Guatemalan municipality of Jilotepeque, about 95 per cent of the Indians in our day have to rent their lands from the mestizos.[59] In such cases conditions prevailing during the colonial period have become completely reversed. The racism pervading nineteenth-century Western civilization strengthened the traditional criollo and mestizo disdain for the "Indian dogs." This attitude helped to keep them apart in an extremely depressed proletarian situation.

Although mestizaje, in the strict sense of the word "miscegenation," had reached practically all the populations of Latin America on the eve

[57] Kubler (1952), 39–42 and *passim*. Sáenz (1933), 262, gives another, earlier example. The governor of Quijos, Peru, reported in 1754 of a village with thirteen mestizos and only two Indian families that "the Mestizos no longer differ from the Indians in color or way of life, for despite being a mixture of whites and Indians, they have retroceded. . . ." According to the governor it was due to their having married Indians, which was probably only a partial explanation.

[58] Stavenhagen (1963), 92. Kubler (1952), 65, concludes: "The colonial attitudes toward passage from Indian to non-Indian caste may be described as more relaxed and more permissive than (it has been) since Independence. . . . The governing factors in the process are probably economic and ideological and in no case biological. . . ."

[59] Stavenhagen (1963), 74.

of the twentieth century, acculturation and assimilation were delayed or even halted in some parts of the immense region. Whereas the multiracial structure of the decaying Régimen de Castas of the late colonial period was rather fluid in practice, the "Indo-American countries" of the nineteenth century brought into being an artificial ethnic dualism between "indígenas" and national citizens. It was a dichotomy with a strong taint of class exploitation.

But let us read a summary of the situation written by Francisco Pimentel, a perspicacious Mexican intellectual, in 1865:

> The white is a proprietor, the Indian a proletarian. The white is rich, the Indian poor, and miserable. The descendants of the Spaniards have all the knowledge of the times within their reach . . . the Indian is ignorant of everything . . . the white lives in the city in a splendid house, the Indian lives in isolation in the countryside in a miserable hut. . . . There are two peoples in the same territory. What is worse, these peoples are to a certain degree mutual enemies.[60]

[60] González de Cossío (1958), 151. It is amusing to find that the Maya Indians also cling to a dualist terminology, the criterion being the place of birth rather than "race." The opposite of the *mazehualob* (natives) are the *dzulob* (aliens). Redfield (1941), 60.

"*Mulato and Mestizo woman sire Quarterón.*" Courtesy of Museo de América, Madrid.

VIII

Negro Slavery

Plantation Slavery in the New World

When the West Indies were discovered, slavery was legally recognized in Spain and Portugal. It was regulated by the famous thirteenth-century Castilian codification, "Las Siete Partidas," though no real distinction was drawn between serf and slave.[1] Increasingly recruited among Negroes from the newly opened territories on the African west coast, slaves had traditionally been employed as domestic servants. But the sixteenth-century commercial revolution brought into being plantations based on slavery, mainly Negro, in the islands occupied by the Iberians off the Atlantic coast: Madeira, the Canaries, Santo Tomé. As a result, slavery, and also the plantation as a slavocrat enterprise, were transferred to the New World.[2]

The plantation can be described as a center specialized in producing and possibly the first stage of processing an item of commercial agriculture. It was intimately bound to the European market, or rather, in the mercantilist era, to the market in the European country that possessed the territory in which the plantation was situated. A long

[1] Gouveia (1960), 76; Davis (1966), 102–103.
[2] Verlinden (1964?), 41.

chain of plantations soon covered the Atlantic coastal areas of the New World from the North American south down to the Brazilian south. In this immense zone, when the Europeans arrived, land was practically a free utility, whereas native population was scarce and primitive. If land is abundant and manpower scarce, permanent labor may be hard to obtain without using some compulsion.[3] Both in Brazil and elsewhere, efforts were at first made to enslave the aborigines for that purpose. But, as we have seen, both Crown and Church, especially in Spanish America, vigorously opposed Indian slavery, though they did not at all object to Negro slavery. How is this ambivalence to be explained? Was it because the suspicion of Moslem faith always hung over the Negroes as a contrast to the "innocence" of Indian paganism? The latter could be won for the True Faith, but the former had already rejected Christianity and deserved harsh punishment. Was it because enslavement seemed less shocking when inflicted upon the human merchandise supplied by African chiefs than in reducing Indians to slavery?[4] The question is an intricate one, but I think Charles Verlinden provides the basic explanation by stating that Indian enslavement was a threat against "colonial peace," whereas the enslavement of Africans, brought from regions where Europeans did not exercise colonial responsibility, did not present a similar threat.[5] If, instead, Africa had first been colonized, perhaps Indian slaves would have been brought to its plantations! In any case, it is historical fact that the Negro slave became the labor force of the plantations in the New World.

Consequently, the plantation zone, selected for geoeconomic reasons, also became Afro-America. Since the plantations provided a common basis for slavery in the North American south, in the Caribbean, and in Brazil, it might have been expected that ethnic relations there would develop similarly in territories of English, Spanish, Dutch, French, and Portuguese tongues. But we know that they did not so develop. The contrast between a common economic basis and later variety in race relations makes the history of the Negro in the New World particularly fascinating and controversial.[6]

[3] Ianni (1962), 81. In Brazil, the possession of slaves was a condition for receiving a land grant (*sesmaria*). Stein (1957), 55–56.

[4] Davis (1966), 169ff.

[5] Verlinden (1964?), *passim*.

[6] The coordinator at the 1957 Seminar on Plantation Systems in the New World concluded: "Recourse must be made to other factors: law, for one, or better . . . religion." PAU (1959), 187.

Religion and Slave Law

We shall not take up the comparative aspects of slavery in different parts of the New World, recently dealt with in a learned work by Cornell historian David Davis.[7] But we cannot ignore those parts of the comparisons presented which have to do with Latin America, even though the analyses of the scholars in question bear traces of being comparative rather than independent. The statement "Slavery was *less* severe in Latin America" characterizes the conclusions and also the assumptions and approach of scholars like Frank Tannenbaum and Stanley Elkins. With the help of Brazil's Gilberto Freyre they explain the difference that has been taken for granted between slavery in Anglo- and Latin America as caused by "national character," religion, and legislation. . . .[8]

The unavoidable vagueness and subjective tone found in any discussion of "national character" makes it unrewarding as a topic for scholarly discussion. Let us, therefore, look instead at the supposedly mitigating influence on slavery of the Church and the Catholic faith in Latin America. In the first place, the Church did not question the validity of Negro slavery and was itself a large-scale slave owner. In 1573, a visionary Spaniard, Bartolomé de Albornoz, daringly challenged several of the basic tenets of slavery, but his treatise was placed on the Index.[9] Some ecclesiastics, like Saint Pedro Claver and Alonso de Sandoval, did what they could to ease the sufferings of the Negro slave in the New World, but their main interest was saving his soul, and they did not question the validity of slavery. If the Jesuits usually treated their slaves relatively well, it would be hard to distinguish their humanitarian reasons from their businesslike understanding of economic expediency. Furthermore, clear evidence of a more humanitarian policy on slavery in Latin America dates from the late eighteenth century and afterward. Since Church and religious influence on politics

[7] Davis (1966).

[8] Freyre (1950, 1963); Tannenbaum (1947); Elkins (1959). A keen early nineteenth-century observer, Depons (1960), I, 110–113, criticized the "traditional view" that Spanish slavery was more humane than the English or French varieties. Admittedly, the masters showed more familiarity toward their slaves and also had them learn a few orations by heart, but slaves were more poorly provided for in food and clothes, he says.

[9] Davis (1966), 189–190.

then reached a low point, the new policy can hardly be said to prove the mitigating influence of Catholicism on slavery.[10] In the same way, the ecclesiastical element took little part in the nineteenth-century abolitionist movements in Latin America.[11] What I have said does not mean that the universalist approach of Catholicism, as distinguished from the exclusivism of many Protestant churches and sects, did not benefit the slaves, but this influence is difficult to measure.[12]

If we pass to the legal aspect, we find that the famed Real instrucción of 1789 on the treatment of slaves in Spanish America clearly represented a fairly humanitarian and even protective approach.[13] But this was the first effort to formulate comprehensive legislation on slavery, and earlier laws governing slavery in Spanish America were mainly repressive, even if more benign passages were not entirely lacking.[14] Legislation in Brazil remained fragmentary and contradictory.[15]

But the important question is, of course, whether whatever there was of humanitarian content in the laws was applied or not. As the North American historian E. G. Bourne wrote as long ago as 1904: "On the relative humanity of the Spanish laws there can be no doubt, but whether Spanish slaves were more kindly treated than French or English is a different and more difficult question." [16] Every student of

[10] *Ibid.*, 227. The recent study by Klein (1966) tries to prove the mitigating influence of the Catholic Church on slavery by comparing conditions in Cuba and Virginia. As E. Gouveia comments, this does not explain the similarity between slavery in the French and in the British West Indies. On the other hand, it was the relatively small percentage of slaves in Cuba and other peculiar local conditions, especially before the breakthrough of the plantation economy there, which permitted a relatively tolerant attitude toward the slaves "which would have been regarded as suicidal by the ruling groups" in the other Caribbean colonies, already fully fledged "plantation colonies." The role of the Church was a secondary one. The attitude of pro-Negro ecclesiastics is best illustrated by Sandoval (1956).

[11] Joaquim Nabuco, Brazilian abolitionist leader, declared that ". . . the Catholic Church . . . never raised its voice in favor of Emancipation (of slaves) in Brazil." Gouveia (1960). See also Stein (1957), 138–139.

[12] Compare with what W. Jiménez Moreno claims in *IPGH* (1961), 82.

[13] *CDFS*, III, 643–652.

[14] A royal decree of 1540, ordering the audiencias to listen to the grievances of slaves who claimed they had the right to freedom, was incorporated in *RI* (1680), VII-V-8. Some seventeenth-century ordinances on the good treatment of slaves are in *HDM*, I, 237–240. Other laws on slavery are in *CDFS*, *passim*.

[15] Boxer (1963), 107.

[16] Bourne (1962), 281. King (1945), 310, states that only the provisions coinciding with the popular attitude toward slavery were carried out.

Latin American colonial history has had ample opportunity to observe how difficult it always was to apply any kind of legislation opposed by some influential group or corporation. Certainly then, it is hard to see how legal norms that restricted the freedom of action of those who owned human property — practically all the influential individuals and corporations in society — could be successful. No less a witness than Alexander von Humboldt also emphasized the impotence of the Spanish authorities in this respect, concluding that "nothing is more illusory than the extolled effects of those laws which prescribe the model of whip or the number of lashes to be given in sequence." [17] The Instruction of 1789 did authorize the priests and special inspectors to gather secret denunciations from the slaves on abuses and bad treatment, and legal documentation has been preserved that the authorities were kept informed about many of the abuses that occurred.[18] But the step from knowledge to efficient action was a very long one.

As the Instruction of 1789 has come to occupy a key position in the discussion, it might be well to keep in mind the context in which it was produced. It is intimately related to the Crown's efforts to extend slavery overseas, and to replace the obsolete system of asientos by free slave trade, assuring a better supply.[19] In most parts of Spanish America until that time, Negro slaves usually had been domestic servants. The Spanish Crown now wanted to make slavery the basis of plantation agriculture according to the French model in Saint Domingue. Naturally enough, the Instruction drew some inspiration from the French *Code Noir* of 1685. If, for partly humanitarian reasons, slavery was somewhat humanized, free Negroes were supposed to serve the same purpose. A preliminary version of the Instruction clearly stressed that it aimed to promote ". . . the useful and assiduous occupation of free Negroes and slaves in the cultivation of articles needed by the metropolis . . ." as well as "the perfect subordination and respect" of both categories "towards civil servants, their masters, and, in general, any white person." [20] Nevertheless, the Instruction's protective features provoked strong opposition in the plantation areas of Spanish America. Even if

[17] Humboldt (1956), II, 105.
[18] Jaramillo Uribe (1963), 23–25, 30–35. The purchase of a slave who suffered from illnesses or vices unknown to the buyer should be legally annulled. As Massini Ezcurra (1961) shows, the records in such cases may illustrate the treatment and the situation of the slaves.
[19] King (1944); Villalobos (1962).
[20] *CDFS*, III, 554–556; Malagón (1956).

it was not repealed, as some students have suggested, there is no reason to believe that the controversial parts of the legal documents have been applied except in rare cases.[21]

Manumission is a special problem of great interest. It has been rather frequent in both Spanish America and Brazil, undoubtedly more so there than in Anglo-America, although the quantitative extent can be established only by painstaking research. In Spanish America there were, by and large, no legal restraints on the owner's right to free his slaves if he wished.[22] Humboldt asserts that, on the contrary, during the last years of the Spanish regime the authorities' policy favored manumission, making use of legal norms prescribing manumission in specific cases, such as cruel treatment.[23] But generalizations about manumission and its effects are likely to be misleading. We have to consider its different forms with their different motivations.

The most frequent category in Latin America probably was purchasing one's freedom.[24] Legally, *all* the produce of slave labor belonged to the proprietor,[25] but by custom and tradition the slave usually was allowed to retain some little saving, the produce of what he cultivated or earned on holidays and the like: in Latin, his *peculium*. This was the basis of self-purchase. An interesting institution was *coartación*, of Cuban origin but later extended to other territories. After the price of self-purchase had been fixed, with or without court arbitration, the pay-

[21] Ortiz (1916), 363, states that the Instruction was not obeyed, but Torre Revello (1932), 42–50, shows that theoretically it remained in force. See also Petit Muñoz (1947), 79–89; Depons (1960), I, 113.

[22] Davis (1966), 262ff., Jaramillo Uribe (1963), 29–30; Depons (1960), I, 114–115; Tannenbaum (1947). A Swedish traveler who visited both the American South and Cuba around 1850 found that Cuban slaves acquired money to purchase their freedom more easily than did slaves in America. On the other hand, Cuban slaves on the plantations were worked harder, their general situation being "much worse." Bremer (1853), III, 109ff.

[23] Humboldt (1941), II, 138–139. Violating the "gentlemen's agreement" between the slaveholders in the Caribbean, the Spanish king in 1773 decided that a number of runaways who arrived in Trinidad from British Tobago and Dutch Essequibo should be set free instead of being restored to their owners; they should be employed as free wage earners. Saco (1938), II, 286–288. It is rather obvious that the Spaniards intended to attract labor from the colonies of the other powers in this way.

[24] Of the manumissions conceded in Mendoza, Argentina, during the first half of the nineteenth century, most were "by purchase" or conditional; only a few were "by grace." Masini (1962), 40. Of 954 cases of manumission in Havana in 1810–1811, 755 were by purchase. Franco (1961), 129.

[25] Davis (1966), 254. In Spanish America, property owned by slaves received legal sanction in 1789. *CDFS*, III, 645–646.

116

ment was made by instalments. If the slave changed masters, the new owner had to respect the coartación, and discount what had already been paid from the price of freedom. The suggestion that slave mothers, in coartación, might also free minor children without additional payment, was rejected by the Council of the Indies in 1788. It did so because this move would have diminished revenues from the sales tax and would imply a reduction in the master's power and control.[26] In Brazil, despite customary manumissions, it was only in 1871 that masters were legally compelled to accept the self-purchase of a slave at his market price.

Purchasing his freedom might benefit others in addition to the slave. Sometimes, a third party advanced the money required in exchange for a promise by the slave to enter into the service of the creditor.[27] In an economic depression, the owner might also find it convenient to offer manumission at a low price, since the slave could neither be advantageously sold to others nor earn his keep.

Free manumission probably was bestowed frequently on old and sick slaves, but this was, of course, anything but humanitarian. The cost of providing for the slave was saved. The Instruction of 1789 justly forbade this type of manumission unless the manumitted were provided with a sufficient peculium.[28] On many occasions, but certainly not always, the lovers and mulatto children of the owner or his sons were also set free. But in 1875, the imperial government of Brazil found it necessary to prohibit the sale of one's own children, indicating that this kind of transaction had not died out.[29] It should not be denied that some wills show that slaves now and then were set free at the owner's death for humanitarian reasons, with expressions of gratitude and appreciation.[30] Our conclusion must be that reasons for granting free manumission varied greatly, making generalizations impossible.

Finally, we have conditional manumission, which often changed the Negro's or the mulatto's situation very little. The same applies to both in-

[26] Aimes (1908–1909); Davis (1966), 266–267; Ortiz (1916), 313; Petit Muñoz (1947), 217–219; CDFS, III, 565–568, 631–635.

[27] Masini (1962), 55–59.

[28] CDFS, III, 647. Potosí chronicler Arzanz y Orsúa (died 1736) also criticized this type of manumission, cxlviii.

[29] Bastide and Fernandes (1955), 99.

[30] A picturesque example of manumission by grace is given by Díaz Soler (1953), 231–232.

dividual manumissions and to those which resulted from abolitionist measures. In Paraguay during the eighteenth century, manumitted slaves were left in charge of some "Spaniard," who paid their tribute to the authorities but then benefited from their work "as if they were his slaves." [31] In Venezuela the Count of Tovar, in the eighteenth century, manumitted a large number of his slaves but made them his tenants. In this way, a Venezuelan historian justly says: "the large landowner . . . liberated himself from the costs of supporting them, and, instead, assured himself of both a fixed annual rent for the land leased out and labor during harvest time." [32]

Slave Labor's Varied Functions

Even in this short survey it becomes clear that current generalizations about slavery in Latin America (often formulated in comparing conditions there with those elsewhere in the New World) suffer from oversimplification and dangerous confusion between legal principles and social reality. That the religion, nationality, and citizenship of a slaveholder made him more or less cruel in his treatment of the slaves has *definitely not* been proved. The objective fact is that slavery is an inhuman institution (even though sanctioned since time immemorial in different cultures), implying the absolute power of one person over another, and absolute power invariably corrupts. But let us see whether another approach will not give us more insight into Negro slavery in its Latin American versions. Analyzing the different functions of slave labor, we discern a number of categories in treatment and opportunities of escape.[33]

The most favored were domestic slaves, kept as servants or even

[31] Carvalho Neto (1962), 44, 49. Those manumitted in accordance with laws of the type *vientre libre* (free womb) were placed, at best, in semifreedom. In Argentina they were even sold "for the years of service fixed by the law." Masini (1962), 53.

[32] Brito Figueroa (1960), 112–113. Sometimes manumission influenced the distribution of negroid population. In Puerto Rico in 1867, the slaves were concentrated in the five centers of plantation agriculture along the coast, whereas the freedmen went inland. Zelinsky (1949), 212–214.

[33] The importance of this approach was realized by Humboldt when he wrote: "What a distance between a slave who serves in the house of a rich man in Havana or Kingston, or who works on his own account . . . and a slave subject to a sugar mill. . . . The [slave] driver of a calash is threatened with the coffee plantation, he who works there with the sugar mill." Quoted by Ortiz (1916), 307.

mainly as tokens of social prestige. The number of Negro footmen who accompanied the owner in the street was more a status symbol than anything else. On the plantation, the domestic slaves, brilliantly portrayed by Freyre, formed the small privileged elite among the unfree mass. Slaves manumitted in wills must usually have been domestics.[34]

Urban slaves, though including many domestic servants, also comprised artisans and skilled workers. The best way of making them profitable was to hire them out or to allow them to work on their own account, obliging them to pay a fixed rent to the owner. Their opportunities of purchasing their freedom were comparatively good, then, but they were subject to great exploitation, especially by poor owners. An American traveler reported from Rio de Janeiro in 1846 that there were "hundreds and hundreds of families [that] have one or two slaves on whose earnings they live." [35] From Caracas a Spanish civil servant reported in 1715 that slaves were sent out by their masters and obliged to earn 2 or 3 reales daily. Since job opportunities were lacking, he says, this turned the men into thieves and the women into prostitutes. That masters used slave women for prostitution is also documented elsewhere.[36]

The cattle *estancia* or cattle ranch also molded slavery in accordance with its function. Slaves could be of real use as cattle hands only if left some freedom of movement and given some trust. Therefore, this category of slaves was relatively well treated, it seems.[37]

On the other hand, mining offered very hard conditions for slave as well as for Indian labor. But Indian labor usually was more abundant and incomparably less expensive, so that Negro slaves were used only in a few mining districts in Latin America. The authorities on one occasion looked at the horribly high mortality figures for the Mita Indians in the mines of Potosí, and suggested that Negro slaves be introduced because their high price would assure them better treatment.

[34] Freyre (1950); Wolff (1964), 166; Arzanz y Orsúa (1965), cxlviii.

[35] Cardozo (1960–1961), 251–252, quoting T. Ewbank. The slaves who were hired out were called *negros de aluguel;* those working on their own, *negros de ganho* in Brazil. Carneiro (1964), 8–10. See also Harth-terré and Márquez Abanto (1962), 46–48. In pearl fishing the same system was employed. Juan and Ulloa (1953), 418–419. For a Spanish parallel, see Domínguez Ortiz (1952), 385–386.

[36] Borges (1963), 138–139. See also Jaramillo Uribe (1963), 32; Santa Gertrudis (1956), I, 44.

[37] Cardoso (1962), 136–139. It was easy to flee from the ranches. Davidson (1966), 251.

That was precisely why Negro labor was never used extensively in the mining district of Alto Peru (presently Bolivia). They were put to use in New Granada (now Colombia) and in Minas Gerais in Brazil. For all their hardships there, they also enjoyed rather good possibilities for saving money that would enable them to buy freedom — if they survived.[38]

In Brazil and in the Spanish Caribbean most slaves were employed in commercial agriculture. Though single slaves were employed on the haciendas in the highlands, mostly as overseers, skilled workers, or artisans, slaves formed the bulk of the labor force only on the plantations on the coast. The relatively high capitalization and profits of the plantations made it possible to use this expensive labor on a larger scale.[39] Working as a field hand was always hard. But it is risky to generalize even about plantation slavery, because the crop, the market conditions, the technology, the capitalization, and other factors modified the life of the slave. With rising capitalization and profits, paternalism, if there ever was any, tended to diminish.[40] Therefore, it seems that the conditions of the slaves in Cuba were worse in 1860 during the sugar boom than they were in 1780 before sugar became dominant. And the deteriorating manpower situation, both enslaved and free labor, in Puerto Rico during the first half of the nineteenth century contrasts with the more favorable conditions in economically depressed Jamaica, where previously there had been an extremely harsh variety of slavery. In nineteenth-century Brazil, the slaves on the *fazendas* of the northeast, with its depressed sugar·economy, apparently enjoyed better conditions than their brethren employed by the dynamic, booming coffee economy in the Paraíba Valley farther south.[41]

The Slave Milieu

The cruel punishments, always normal in the plantation environment, should mainly be explained as arising from the mutual fear of masters and slaves. It is strange that the economic self-interest of the

[38] Boxer (1962), 173–178; Wolff (1964), 163–164; Jaramillo Uribe (1963). When mining declined in Minas Gerais, there were large-scale manumissions. Carneiro (1964), 25.
[39] Wolf and Mintz (1957), 390, define haciendas and plantations.
[40] Harris (1965), 45.
[41] Morse (1964), 9; Mintz (1959), 273–281; Stein (1957), *passim.*

owner did not save many slaves from being put to death. Making this same observation, Humboldt mentions a planter in Curiaco, Venezuela, who flogged two of his eight slaves to death and soon lost another four by his careless treatment.[42] But the excessive work to which slaves were subjected was caused by the structure of the plantation economy. The slaves often represented more than half the total investment in a plantation; an inelastic investment that was profitable only when they were kept working.[43] The rate of reproduction of the slaves was very low, probably because of psychological factors,[44] but also because of the bad treatment suffered by pregnant slave women. The systematic "slave breeding" in Virginia and South Carolina for the cotton belt plantations farther to the southwest [45] seems to have had no counterpart in Latin America. As long as it was possible to replenish the stock of slaves by importing them or by purchasing them from other owners, the slavocrats of Latin America preferred to do so rather than promote slave reproduction and the lost days of work by pregnant women and the like that it implied. The short-sightedness of the slave owners of south-central Brazil is reflected in the calculation of an average "durability" of the slave newly arrived in the plantations around 1850: about ten years.[46] If this figure is correct, conditions were really horrible.

The lack or weakness of family and community bonds among the slaves was, of course, the intended result of slavery. The lack of balance between the sexes continued. In the coffee district in the Paraíba Valley, studied by Stanley Stein, 77 per cent of the slaves in the 1820's were men.[47] It was only in 1869 that the separate sale of husband,

[42] Humboldt (1956), V, 105–106. In the words of Jaramillo Uribe (1963), 31, ". . . New Granadan slavocrat society was filled with tensions, conflicts and hatred." The cruelty was documented by scars on slave bodies, etc. in Freyre (1963b), 220. Possibly slavery in Brazil became more repressive during the latest period. Cardoso (1962), 272. From Argentina, on the contrary, the Swede Graaner (1949) reported in 1816: "In respect of the slaves, the American Spaniard is, perhaps, too lenient to the degree that slaves are seen rubbing elbows with their masters, above all since the slave trade was completely discontinued. . . ."

[43] Stein (1957), 225.

[44] Cf. T. Mathews in *IPGH* (1961), 94. Even in well-administered haciendas, the reproduction rate of the slaves seems to have lagged behind that of free Negroes. Garzón Maceda and Dorflinger (1962).

[45] On this topic, see Conrad and Meyer (1964), 43–114.

[46] Straten Ponthoz (1854), III, 116. Cf. Davis (1966), 232–233.

[47] Stein (1957), 76–77, 155–156; Aguirre Beltrán in *PAU* (1957), 70. In Minas Gerais there were 117,171 Negro men but only 49,824 women in 1776.

wife, and minor children was prohibited, but even then the marriage of a slave required the owner's previous permission.[48] Under these circumstances, miscegenation between masters and slave women necessarily occurred everywhere Negroes were held in bondage. How distinctive Brazilian or other Latin American plantations were in this respect is difficult to say, and it is not a very interesting question. It is clear that the master's abuse of the women under his control has nothing whatsoever to do with a lack of racial prejudice on his part,[49] as influential authors have tried to make us believe. The same applies to his religion. Sexual relationships on the plantations of Dutch Calvinist Surinam were only too similar to those in Catholic Portuguese northeast Brazil.[50] To deny that plantation promiscuity was unique for Latin America is not to deny its importance. The children born in master-slave unions were often, but, as we have stressed, certainly not always, manumitted. Sexual relationships also created a web of subtle links between the master's house (or *Casa Grande* on the Brazilian fazenda) and the slaves' hut (or *senzala*), never better described than in Gilberto Freyre's works.

More or less abandoned by the Church, the plantation world witnessed the growth of a peculiar syncretist religion, but otherwise the slavocrat system imposed a filter which very few African traditions were able to penetrate.[51] Food for subsistence apparently was produced on the plantation itself or imported, according to economic expediency.[52] The plantation economy was intimately linked with other regional and foreign economies. The not very tasty jerked beef of Rio Grande do Sul in Brazil and of Spanish-speaking Río de la Plata was destined for the stomachs of Brazilian slaves. Fernando Henrique Cardoso has described the inhuman conditions of slave labor in the *charqueadas* or salting plants of Rio Grande do Sul. This merciless exploitation illustrates the inherent weakness of the slavocrat system in the nineteenth

Machado Filho (1943), 25. Poor slave owners often held only a couple of male slaves, since work in the home was done by the housewife. Cardoso and Ianni (1960), 29, 68–69.

[48] Bastide and Fernandes (1955), 98.

[49] Well expressed by Harris (1964), 68.

[50] Lier (1949).

[51] See, e.g., Warren (1965) and Aguirre Beltrán in *PAU* (1957), 67.

[52] Cf. Harris (1964), 46; Stein (1957), 47–48; S. Mintz in *American Anthropologist*, LXIII (1961), 585.

century. Competing with the plants in Río de la Plata which used wage labor, the charqueadas of Rio Grande declined more and more. Having more incentive, two free workers equaled three slaves. Furthermore, the risky investment in the life of a slave (with a very low expectancy of reproduction) was much heavier than the cost of wages.[53] Therefore, slavocrat systems could defend themselves only in mutual competition, as, for a long time, in sugar production. Although in the British West Indies slavery helped to create the capital needed for British industrialization, as demonstrated by Eric Williams, once industrial capitalism was established, slavery increasingly became an economic as well as a social anomaly.[54]

Toward Abolition

The radical change in the British attitude toward the slave traffic and slavery itself during the early nineteenth century thus obeyed complex economic, political, and humanitarian motivations. Having forbidden English subjects to engage in slave trading in 1807, Great Britain soon tried to force other nations to follow her example. The result, in Latin America, was a long series of treaties between the new nations and Great Britain aimed at abolishing the importation of slaves.[55] In some cases, the contracting Spanish American countries had already decreed abolition themselves or at least initiated the process of abolition. But resistance was met in those countries where slavery still was economically important: Peru, Spain (representing Cuba), and, above all, Brazil. After resisting increased British pressure for many years, the imperial government of Brazil finally suppressed the slave traffic by the law of Eusébio de Quiroz in 1850. A Brazilian student has put forward the explanation that this law became politically feasible and was enforced because it implied that the debts that landowners had incurred with slave suppliers would be suspended.[56] The disruption of the slave trade meant eventual doom for slavery, because of the low rate of reproduction in the slave population, but it was not extinguished for another two decades in Cuba and for thirty-eight years in Brazil. Dur-

[53] Cardoso (1962), *passim*.
[54] Williams (1944).
[55] King (1944).
[56] Carneiro (1964), 91–94.

ing the 1850's, slavery was abolished in Venezuela, Colombia, Ecuador, and Peru. Abolition was also completed in Argentina and Uruguay. In Mexico, Central America, and Chile, slavery had already disappeared. In Brazil the process was slow, taking place by stages: the law of Rio Branco freeing the slave children born after September 28, 1871; the Law of the Sexagenarians in 1885; and universal abolition without compensation to the owners on the glorious *Treze de Maio* (Thirteenth of May), 1888. In a convincing way, a recent student has related this process to the economic and social transformation in Brazilian society during this period, and also has emphasized how important the large-scale slave desertions from the coffee plantations, encouraged by urban abolitionists, were in bringing about final abolition.[57] The slave population has been calculated at 1,107,000 in 1819, 1,510,000 in 1872, 1,272,000 in 1882, and only 637,000 in 1887.[58] The importation of slaves during the first half of the nineteenth century, despite British efforts to curb it, seems to have reached between 750,000 and 1 million individuals.[59] Especially during the last decade, when it was evident that slavery was dying, manumissions were frequent. In Brazil, the suspension of the slave trade with Africa was followed by an intensification of internal slave trade, by which slaves from the decaying northeast were sold to the prosperous coffee planters of the Paraíba Valley.[60]

Let us summarize the conclusions we have reached on the intricate and controversial topic of slavery in Latin America. Its character in that region, as elsewhere, seems mainly to have been determined by the slave's economic function. Consequently, plantation slavery has in the

[57] Graham (1966). One of the leading abolitionists in São Paulo, Luis Gama, was a mulatto who himself had been a slave. After six years in the army he became a civil servant and poet. Morse (1958), 146. On the other hand, a leading antiabolitionist in Brazil, Domingo Carlos Silva, was also colored. Freyre (1959), I, 322.

[58] Stein (1957), 295.

[59] Observing that the slave population of the United States increased during the same period despite less extensive importation, Furtado (1959), 141–143, suggests that conditions of slaves in Brazil might have been worse. In Cuba the slave population increased from 84,690 in 1792 to 199,145 in 1817, but legal importation during that period was no fewer than 147,483 individuals. Even allowing for a certain amount of manumission and re-export, these figures suggest a high death rate among slaves, Zelinsky (1949), 206.

[60] Cardoso (1962), 80–81; Bastide and Fernandes (1955), 36. On the evolution of prices during this period, Stein (1957), 65, 228; Carneiro (1964), 59–62.

main the same characteristics throughout the Americas. If slavery in a Latin American environment appeared to be "mild," the explanation usually will be found in the existing socioeconomic structure. Also, the character and extent of manumission generally reflected socioeconomic conditions.

"Negro dance," a Chinese drawing on rice paper in a manuscript from about 1860 belonging to the "Lipperheideschen Kostümbibliothek" (Md 20) in the Kunstbibliothek, Berlin. The artist probably was a coolie who had returned from Peru to Canton.

A Peruvian Indian woman leading a llama, by the Chinese artist who drew "Negro dance." Courtesy of the Kunstbibliothek, Berlin.

IX

Race Distribution and Race Relations Since the Mid-1800's

An Ethnic Map of Modern Latin America

Latin American society has undergone a profound transformation in the last hundred years. Both external factors such as the mid-nineteenth century technological and economic revolution and internal factors such as population growth have contributed to change. Both immigration and internal migrations have changed the ethnic composition of the population. A society of economic classes has developed and industrial capitalism has grown, strongly influencing values and attitudes, and these are important also in ethnic relations. But it is difficult to trace even in broad outline the new or, rather, the modified pattern of race distribution and racial attitudes, because few serious studies have been done on the social history of the last hundred years. Most of the works by anthropologists and sociologists, naturally enough, lack historical perspective.

As the national period began, the Indians were already in the minority compared with the population of Latin America as a whole. The mestizos dominated in the peripheral parts of Mexico, in Central America south of Guatemala, in most of Venezuela and Colombia, in the strip along the Pacific coast of South America, in the whole of Chile, and also east of the Andes in Argentina, Uruguay, Paraguay, and parts of southern and central Brazil. But, as we have pointed out, considerable Indian populations also lived along with the mestizos in almost all of Spanish America and great parts of Brazil. The greatest part of the Negro population lived, of course, in the plantation zone along the Atlantic coast from Rio de Janeiro to Cartagena in the West Indies. In Cuba they were concentrated in the western part. Many also lived in the interior of Mexico and Colombia as well as along the Pacific coastal strip in Ecuador and Peru.[1]

During the national period, the indigenous population has been reduced to more or less extensive pockets in the western and southern parts of Mexico, northern Guatemala, the highlands of Ecuador, Peru, and Bolivia, plus the small clusters that still exist in parts of the Amazon basin. The border between the highland "Indians" and the rest of the population is sociocultural rather than racial. A great part of the land that a hundred years ago still belonged to mestizo Latin America has been completely transformed by European immigration. This applies to Argentina (except, perhaps, for parts of the Andean provinces), Uruguay, southernmost Chile, and southern Brazil. All these territories are in the temperate zone and thus particularly attractive to European settlers. But European immigration has also modified the population of Cuba, Puerto Rico and, in more recent times, Venezuela. In Afro-Latin America during the last century, the negroid population in northeastern Brazil and along the Caribbean coast of Central America has expanded. Practically the whole of the West Indies is dominated by Negroes, although their share in the population of Cuba and Puerto Rico has steadily diminished. In Mexico, where there were still many Negroes a hundred years ago, they have been almost entirely absorbed. After Negro slavery was abolished, the plantations' demand for docile manpower caused the immigration of contract labor, mostly of Asiatic origin, as will be shown in greater detail below. Thus new ethnic categories were added to the already pluralistic pattern of Negroes, mulattoes, and whites in the plantation zone of Latin America.

Since we have dealt with the changing relations between mestizos and indígenas in the highlands, we shall concentrate in this chapter on the changes that have occurred in the plantation or the torrid lowland zone. We shall also briefly comment on the effects of European immigration.

[1] A good survey of the negroid population is in Zelinsky (1949). See also Rosenblat (1954).

Abolition's Effect on Plantation America

In the plantation zone, the natural point of departure is the abolition of Negro slavery. The extent to which abolition changed the distribution of the Negro population was determined principally by the existence or lack of other jobs, including the availability of land fit for subsistence agriculture. In Colombia, many Negro freedmen drifted into the Magdalena Valley, for example, finding jobs as woodcutters and oarsmen.[2] In northern Brazil, abolition was followed by mass flights from the plantations and general disturbances, but this state of things did not last for long. Many owners of slaves had believed that the "gratitude" of the former slaves would easily turn them into wage earners. But it was hardly "gratitude" that made the Negroes of the northeast return to the plantations — it was the lack of alternatives in a zone bordering on the dry *caatinga* or scrubforest and already occupied by large estates. Therefore, the plantations in this zone seem to have recovered rapidly all the manpower they needed, considering the diminution in the demand for labor that resulted when the industry was modernized. In the Paraíba Valley, the new wage labor was established rapidly enough to save even the harvest of 1888.[3] In São Paulo and the south there were plenty of jobs during this period of expansion, but also European immigrants were offering increasing competition. The Negroes were handicapped by their lack of training. It was believed by most abolitionists in Brazil and the rest of Latin America that political justice would automatically bring about socioeconomic justice as well. When abolition came, almost no preparations had been made in Brazil and elsewhere to train the new citizens for their functions in order to integrate them with society.[4] Only the army readily accepted them and trained them for a new task. "The destiny of the Negro in our country was to pass from slavery to the barracks," a Uruguayan historian declares, and that was also true in other countries where Negroes were few.[5] Some of the Negroes in southern Brazil

---

[2] James (1950), 106.

[3] Furtado (1959), 164–165; Stein (1957), 264–265. The presence of industrious Negro tenants in the Reconcavo area near Bahia since abolition should also be noticed. James (1950), 390.

[4] Cf. Freyre (1959), I, 329.

[5] Pereda Valdés (1941), 129. Similar conditions prevailed in Argentina. Many colored Brazilian troops took part in the Paraguayan War (1865–1870).

managed to become workers and sharecroppers but many, succumbing to competition, turned to subsistence agriculture or to a completely marginal existence. There and elsewhere, the situation of many Negro freedmen was evidence of their lack of professional training and the brutalizing, degrading effects of slavery.[6]

In turn, the marginal existence led by many freedmen helped to strengthen ethnic prejudice against the Negro. Ethnic prejudice during the postabolition period fulfilled the same function in Brazil and some Spanish American countries as in the United States, maintaining the abyss between white and black that used to be automatically assured by the master-slave dichotomy. In other words, the existing social inequality was justified by reference to a supposed racial inequality. Such external factors as European racism and, in southern Brazil, European immigration, added to the prejudice.[7] Many Brazilians found in immigration the remedy to the "racial" problem. The governor of Parana stated in 1888 that immigration ought to be "an ethnic factor of primary importance destined to strengthen the national body, bastardized by the vice of origin and its contact with slavery." [8] That prejudice was more apparent in southern Brazil than in the north is not difficult to explain. In the north, the Negro's condition remained almost the same, whereas in the south, transformed by immigration and an economic boom, the Negroes were one of the groups competing for jobs. As we have emphasized, prejudice does not necessarily express itself in rigid forms of discrimination, and the forms that have emerged in Brazil have been extralegal, subtle, and vague. Thus it has been possible to

[6] For an exhaustive study on postabolition conditions in São Paulo, see Fernandes (1965). See also Bastide and Fernandes (1955), 120–121. In Puerto Rico, on the contrary, former slaves often obtained better jobs in sugar mills than others. Mintz (1951), 239–240, 246–247.

[7] Cardoso and Ianni (1960), 236; Cardoso (1962); Ianni (1962), 244–247; Fernandes (1965), *passim*; Bastide and Fernandes (1955), 363–367. Notice how prejudice was modified depending on whether Negroes or mulattoes were concerned. Freyre (1959), I, 306, states that an academic career helped many mulattoes to overcome their racial handicap, providing them with "charters of sociological whiteness." It is interesting that in midcentury Buenos Aires Negro freedmen put up a fight against racial inequality. Their mouthpieces were the papers *La Raza Africano o sea el Demócrata Negro* and *El Proletario*. Rodríguez Molas (1961), 119.

[8] Ianni (1962), 264. Sometimes the immigrants and their descendants adopted racist attitudes. When talking to a "German" mayor in a small town in Rio Grande do Sul in 1950, I heard him refer to a bypasser (light mulatto) with the disdainful words (in German): "Those blue people called Brazilians."

create the "racial democracy" myth in a country where, in fact, the miserable majority of the very dark-skinned is contrasted to the prosperous, overwhelmingly "white" elite.[9]

Forced labor within the plantation economy did not disappear with abolition. We know, for instance, that even when slavery still existed in Spanish Puerto Rico, "free" proletarians were put into forced labor by laws directed against "vagrancy." [10] This device probably was often used elsewhere as well. When the supply of Negro slaves was cut off, plantation interests lay behind the only slightly more humane trade in Asiatic coolies. Between 1849 and 1874, Peru imported about 80,000 Chinese, contracted for work on the sugar plantations and extracting guano in the Chincha islands. They were so badly treated as to give rise to international scandals and diplomatic complications between Peru and China.[11] Between 1847 and 1867, another 114,000 Chinese arrived in Cuba. Subject to the same abuses as in Peru, many Chinese took part in the Cuban rebellion against the Spanish regime in 1868. This, in turn, caused the traffic to be suspended by the Spanish authorities.[12] In the second half of the century, hundreds of thousands of Asiatics immigrated into Guiana and other European possessions in the Caribbean, coming from both China and India.[13] Even if usually

[9] "Color prejudice, the mysticism of the whitening, the myth of arianization, the myth of racial democracy are all products of the critical phase of disorganization and reorganization of the social system as this is being affected by the transformation of labor." Ianni (1962), 265. Freyre (1959), II, 352–382, records interviews in which race was discussed with 183 Brazilians born during the latter half of the nineteenth century and representing different regions and strata (though heavily elite). Though some are frankly racist, most state their positive view of the colored. But when asked how they would react if their daughter or some other family member wanted to marry a colored man, most either evaded the question or admitted to a negative reaction. Some were completely aware of the contradiction. As one Paulista born in 1888 stated, referring to his sincere belief in racial tolerance but lack of enthusiasm in having family ties with coloreds: "There are in me invincible forces due to ancestry that justify this attitude. They are, I understand, instinctive rather than rational. . . ." (II, 359–360).

[10] Mintz (1951). In Venezuela police regulations helped to restrict the freedom of the freedmen. Lombardi (1967), 22.

[11] Stewart (1951). Ruthless traders also started a traffic in Polynesian slaves to provide the guano enterprisers with manpower. Fortunately, French and Hawaiian authorities soon succeeded in stopping this attempt. Véliz (1961), 147–156.

[12] Chang-Rodríguez (1958), 375–399; Jiménez Pastrana (1963). It reveals the misery of slaves and semislaves that of 346 cases of suicide registered in Cuba in 1862, 173 were Chinese and 130 Negro slaves. Ortiz (1916), 392.

[13] Bastien (1964), 181.

not replacing Negro labor in the plantations, the coolies helped the plantation owners to maintain low wages. Imported contract workers, of any race, were preferred to native workers because they were more easily disciplined and controlled.[14]

In the south of Brazil, Italians and other poor Europeans took the Negroes' place on the coffee fazendas. From the management point of view, the color of the skin did not matter; the Italians were so vilely treated that in 1902 the Italian government prohibited further emigration to the State of São Paulo.[15] It was only from this time onward that Asiatic immigration to Brazil became important. It culminated between 1926 and 1941. Up to 1941, almost 190,000 Japanese had found their way to Brazil, and 29,000 went to Peru. Many of the Japanese were natives of the Ryukyu islands, especially Okinawa. After World War II, migration from these islands started again. About 2,500 Ryukyuans have established agricultural colonies in the Bolivian lowlands. In São Paulo and the neighboring states, many of the independent farmers are Japanese. The Nisei (those born in Brazil), however, show a tendency to drift to cities.[16] In Peru, most descendants of the coolies have been absorbed by the urban middle strata.

The acculturation and assimilation of the Asiatics is rather peculiar. Among the immigrants, the lack of balance between the sexes was often extreme. The coolies were exclusively male, which inevitably produced miscegenation. On the other hand, the Asiatics offered especially vigorous cultural and religious resistance to intermarriage and assimilation. Thus, very different phenomena have occurred. The coolies imported to Peru, besides being all males, were kept isolated from other people during the time of their contract. This led inevitably to some homosexuality, which, when discovered, strengthened prejudices against the poor Asiatics.[17] Later, they mixed with Peruvian women, creating a very attractive human type, the *injertos* and *injertas* of Lima. Among the Ryukyuans of Bolivia, no less than two-thirds of the marriages are mixed, at the same time a symptom and a partial explanation for this group's high degree of assimilation. But the marriages of the first Japanese in Brazil with caboclas often failed because of the cultural distance. The Japanese found the women inferior. As

[14] Wolf and Mintz (1957), 400; Dahl (1960/1961), 35.
[15] Bastide and Fernandes (1955), 78–79.
[16] Saito (1961); Irie (1951/1952); Tigner (1963); Mörner (1960).
[17] Stewart (1951), 103, 230.

soon as Japanese women arrived they married them instead. An endogamous pattern brought back the traditional Japanese family, in which the parents arranged marriages. The lack of assimilation was the backdrop of Japanese nationalist movements in Brazil during and immediately after World War II.[18]

In the plantation zone the ethnic map has been greatly modified because of internal migrations, impelled mainly by economic factors. Toward the end of the nineteenth century, when banana plantations were established along the Caribbean coast of Central America, the manpower brought into this sparsely populated zone was supplied by Negroes from Jamaica and the Bahamas.[19] When many banana plantations in eastern Costa Rica were destroyed by the *sigatoka* disease, the Negroes became unemployed but reverted to subsistence agriculture.[20] The construction of the Panama canal created numerous jobs for West Indian Negroes, who usually stayed in Panama. One result of the canal's opening in 1914 was the prosperity of the Cauca Valley in southeastern Colombia and the growth of its seaport Buenaventura. This city, as well as Cartagena and its younger sister harbor on the Atlantic, Barranquilla, are predominantly Negro.[21] In the West Indies, manpower has moved from island to island in accordance with occasional or seasonal demand for labor. Between 1916 and 1935, 150,000 Haitians are reported to have gone to Cuba as farm laborers during the *zafra* or sugar harvest season. Many stayed there.[22] Haitian workers of the same category were the victims of the giant massacre ordered by the Dominican despot Trujillo in 1937.

Immigration in the Temperate Regions

Previously mainly mestizo, the temperate zone of southern South America received most of the twelve million European immigrants who arrived in Latin America between 1850 and 1930.[23] But about 40 per cent returned sooner or later to their native lands. Since Argentina,

[18] Tigner (1961, 1963).
[19] See, e.g., Dahl (1960/1961); González Navarro (1957), 166–172. After the uprising in Yucatán in 1847, Maya "slaves" were exported to Cuba. Franco (1961), 108.
[20] James (1950), 660.
[21] *Ibid.*, 99–100.
[22] Bastien (1964), 182.
[23] Short accounts by Humphreys (1946), Mörner (1960).

133

Uruguay, and the south of Brazil formerly were very sparsely populated, the enormous waves of newcomers soon outnumbered the original population, although they gradually adopted at least part of the criollo tradition and also the language of the land. Most of the immigrants were from Italy, Spain, and Portugal, so that assimilation was comparatively easy. The whole zone now took on a European appearance and the Negro element in both Argentina and Uruguay definitively disappeared.

The history of European immigration is rather little known despite its basic importance for the Latin American countries mainly affected. Especially little is known of relations between immigrants and the native population. The sex ratio evidently has been the major determinant of race mixture caused by the new immigration, as it was in the sixteenth century among the Iberian immigrants. In southernmost Brazil, the Germans who had settled there during the first half of the nineteenth century usually brought their families along. Therefore, they had less need for intermarriage with other groups. In fact, the "German" population has grown rapidly in this zone mainly because of a high rate of reproduction together with tenacious resistance against assimilation.[24] On the other hand, male predominance among the migrants necessarily led to more extensive miscegenation and intermarriage, which naturally quickened the rate of assimilation. The immigration into Argentina between 1857 and 1926 was 71 per cent male and about two thirds were adults under 40 years of age. Victor Raúl Haya de la Torre exclaimed: "Today a new Mestizaje is emerging in Latin America" at a meeting on the history of race mixture held in Stockholm, Sweden, in 1960 — both the Asiatic and European immigrations provided abundant examples to support his view.[25]

Most of the newly arrived immigrants were poor, so that they had to find their first sexual partners among the lower strata of society. In the Latin American environment, this meant, often, that those partners were of dark skin. According to Gilberto Freyre, the poor European immigrants often joined mulatto women, appealing not only because of their sexual attractiveness, but also their willingness to support the

[24] Willems (1946), 451–462; Roche (1959), 455–472. As to the Italians in the same zone, a similar tendency prevails. From 1912 to 1954, interethnic marriage in one parish of the area amounted only to 5 per cent. Azevedo (1961), 66.
[25] IPGH (1961), 199.

newcomers. As washerwomen or cooks, the mulatto women were able to do so. At the same time, Freyre admits that the children born to these unions faced a double handicap, owing to their descent from European "trash" and Africans.[26] In Paraguay, I have met several people of very modest standing who were the offspring of unions between German or English adventurers and native women, people with blue eyes and blond hair who spoke only Guaraní. So it is and always will be everywhere in Latin America when immigrants and visitors take to the women of the country, cases of miscegenation which do not even modify the local culture. But when immigration triggered acculturation, the phenomenon worked both ways. Whereas the "Europeanizing" effects have been obvious and frequently stressed in scholarly literature, many European immigrants, especially those living in the rural areas, underwent profound transformations, brought on by the environment and competition with native labor. In a literary work, *The Jewish Gauchos of the Pampas*, Gerchunoff described, better than any scholar, this process in his story of ten thousand exiles from the ghettos of Russia who tried their luck as farmers in the province of Santa Fé, Argentina. On the German, Italian, and Polish colonization in southern Brazil, a distinguished student has recently emphasized the importance of the new settlers' acculturation in a primitive environment.[27] How different religious and other concepts as to family and morals have affected relations between the immigrants, particularly those from non-Latin European countries, and the native Latin Americans, is an interesting though little-known subject. Incidentally, immigration to the temperate zone of Latin America has not been exclusively European. A large number of immigrants from the Near East, known as "Turcos" and Syrio-Lebanese, have found their way to almost every part of Latin America. Their assimilation has met with no major problems. After all, their phenotypes are very similar to those of other Mediterranean peoples.[28]

In the temperate zone also, internal migrations have modified the ethnic map, though less than in the plantation zone. In the Argentine northwest, Bolivian migrants have strengthened the Indian streak in

[26] Freyre (1951), I, 345 and *passim*. See also Freyre (1959), I, 334–336. A parallel phenomenon in eighteenth-century Cartagena is described by Juan and Ulloa (1768), I, 37–38.

[27] Waibel (1955). A. Gerchunoff's book, in an English edition, 1955.

[28] The assimilation of the Near Easterners has manifested itself in, among other things, participation in national politics. See Bray (1962).

the population; in the northeast, Paraguayan mestizos have settled down in an area otherwise housing a most cosmopolitan population of European immigrants. Both categories, of course, have been attracted primarily by better employment opportunities.[29] The populations of the slums in Argentine cities, especially Buenos Aires, have been swelled by mestizo elements from the Andean provinces. In other countries, such as Peru, where the urban population is heavily mestizo, the influx from the countryside into the slums has in part been indigenous and by and large has represented a darker shade of skin.

Varied Race Relations in the Americas

We have already noticed the strengthening of ethnic prejudice in Afro-Latin America following abolition. The European immigration into the temperate zone similarly affected the few remaining elements of color there. In Indo-Latin America, during the national period, the indigenous population became more and more isolated, as already described. Nevertheless, a comparison with race relations in the United States, for example, will show a striking difference. There can be no doubt that these relations are smoother and more humane in almost any Latin American environment than are those in the United States, even outside Mississippi and Alabama. But there is also a very obvious difference between race relations in Indo-Latin America and in Afro-Latin America. In the former we find a genetically artificial, ethnic dualism between indígenas and others, which corresponds to the dualism between so-called whites and so-called Negroes in the United States. But, whereas the criterion in Anglo-America is genealogical, founded on what is known about the descent of a person and rigidly excluding anybody with some African ancestry from white status, the criterion in Indo-Latin America is sociocultural and thus much more bland and fluid. "Passing" may simply be a question of buying a European dress and of moving to another place. Finally, in Afro-Latin America, with its racial pluralism, the criterion for distinguishing the different groups is physical appearance, the phenotype, but it is somewhat modified by social and cultural considerations. If a dark person is cultured and prosperous, society will somehow find his skin a shade lighter. Thus, "passing" is also somewhat easier there than in the rigid

[29] For oral information on the Bolivian immigration I am obliged to Professor Germán Tjarks. I have visited Argentine Misiones myself.

136

and exclusivist Anglo-Saxon environment. Whereas "mulatto," at least in the United States today, is the really offensive word, "Negro" is a word to be avoided in Brazil. It seems certain that the difference in attitudes between the two societies was especially profound with reference to the mulatto and the realization of or refusal to realize that miscegenation is a historical fact.[30]

These differences between race relations in Anglo-America and Afro-Latin America are hard to explain, but it must be obvious from our account in Chapter VIII that the explanation is not to be found in the conditions of plantation slavery. Probably the different ways in which abolition was attained have more to do with the problem. In the United States, abolitionism was a vigorous, popular movement that, however, attained its goal only after a devastating civil war. In the Caribbean, on the contrary, abolition was imposed from above. In Brazil, it was the end result of a very lengthy process, in which both external and internal factors were active. Even so, final abolition helped cause the most stable government in nineteenth-century Latin America to fall. Perhaps the vigor of humanitarianism in the United States rather than its weakness helps to explain the reactionary and brutal attitude of white racists in the American South.[31]

Another, even more important circumstance has been indicated by anthropologist Marvin Harris. Even prior to Negro slavery there were many poor whites in the North American South, and the emancipated Negroes had to compete with them. In Latin America, the corresponding stratum was the result of three centuries of miscegenation. The gradual absorption of these people, first those manumitted and later those freed by abolition, caused less tension.[32] Like Latin America, the societies founded by North Europeans in the Caribbean recognized the mulattoes as an intermediate stratum. But existing variations in racial relations in the Caribbean, with its relatively similar economic structure and cultural diversity, show just how complex the problem is. A sociologist suggested recently that the physical distance between the North European and the Negro or mulatto actually is, and is felt to be, much greater than that between the Mediterranean white and the people of

[30] ". . . the main practical difference between Anglo-American and Latin American race attitudes is the position of the Mulatto rather than the Negro. . . ." W. J. Cahnman, quoted by Hoetink (1961), 633.
[31] Harris (1964), 93–94.
[32] Stein (1964), 16; Harris (1964), 83–89.

African admixture, and that this distance has helped mold race relations in the Caribbean.[33] This would not be surprising at all.

But the historian who has to cope with comparative race relations must find himself at a loss when trying to reach beyond tangible explanations of the differences between the predominant patterns in various areas. The study of ethnic attitudes is properly within the social psychologist's domain. And we are still waiting for a convincing interpretation of the contrasts that I have been discussing from these quarters.

Generalizations on ethnic attitudes in various parts of Latin America are sometimes far from valid. Racial conflict may arise from economic competition and as a violent expression of accumulated ethnic prejudice among the "majority group," taking on remarkably similar characteristics in different environments. Thus, the Chinese, a hardworking, only partly assimilated group, faced almost identical kinds of persecution in the western United States and northern Mexico. A massacre in Torreón in 1911 cost three hundred Chinese their lives. In 1931, a lengthy story of discrimination against the Chinese in Sonora culminated in a decree by the state government forbidding the Chinese, among other things, to marry Mexican women, even when the "Chinese" in question was a Mexican citizen. This decree caused the collective exodus of the Chinese from Sonora, the economic life of which was injured as a result.[34] Such episodes show that, under certain conditions, latent ethnic prejudice may rapidly produce discrimination and racial violence in any ethnic environment. It is not a phenomenon unique to Anglo-Saxons, Germans, and South Africans.

[33] Hoetink (1961), 638. Thesis presented with more detail in his "De gespelten samenleving in het Caribisch gebied" (Assen, 1962).
[34] Cumberland (1960). For discriminatory immigration laws of the Latin American countries with reference to Asiatics see Bradley (1942), 67–68. See also González Navarro (1957), 166–172.

X

The Indian's Renaissance and Race Mixture Re-evaluated

Racism

In Latin American romantic literature, both the Indian, and, somewhat less frequently, the Negro are represented.[1] The first author to approach the topic with some realism and awareness of the misery of the dark-skinned was a Peruvian woman, Clorinda Matto de Turner, who in 1889 published her *Aves sin nido* (*Birds Without Nests*), which had no great literary value, by the way. Until the beginning of the twentieth century, social justice for Indians and Negroes found few literary champions.[2] A little earlier, however, the dark-skinned people began at least to be considered a social problem and even a cause behind Latin America's slow development. After 1883, when Domingo Faustino Sarmiento published his book *Conflictos y armonías de las razas en América* (*Conflict and Harmony Between the Races in America*), the "racial" factor was more and more often discussed. The subject was approached from positivist and Spencerian (or Social Darwinist) points of view, the philosophies then in vogue. European racism, as preached

[1] Meléndez (1934); Manzoni (1939); Sayers (1956).
[2] Zum Felde (1959), II, 254–256.

by Count Gobineau,[3] Vacher de Lapouge, Houston Chamberlain, and Gustave Le Bon also left their mark.[4] At that time, we must realize, racist ideas seemed to represent modern science. Anthropometrics, for instance, was considered a special discipline. If we think of the extreme sensitivity of the Latin Americans toward everything that was in vogue in Paris, it is remarkable that racism was not even more strongly influential among Latin American intellectuals. In Mexico, most of the *científicos*, the positivist intellectuals gathered around Dictator Porfirio Díaz, accepted race mixture as a historical fact, but pinned their hopes on the positive influence of popular education. Both Gabino Barreda and Justo Sierra argued that the Indian was educable. Among the principal científicos, only Francisco Bulnes was an outspoken, though confused, racist. He compared the vigor and intelligence of North Europeans, who lived on a wheat diet, with the weakness of Amerindians and Orientals, nurtured by corn and rice. But he did not reach the logical conclusion of his argument: the difference should be resolved simply by a change in the diet! [5] Outside Mexico, more racist influence can be found. Take the rhetoric of Argentine Carlos Octavio Bunge, son of a German immigrant, speaking of the mestizos and mulattoes in 1903: "Both are impure, atavistically anti-Christian; they are like the two heads of a fabulous hydra that surrounds, constricts and strangles with its giant spiral a beautiful, pale virgin, Spanish America. . . ." [6] Bunge had many readers at the time. For him and others of the same tendency, the fact of miscegenation provided, of course, an easy explanation for all the tragedies in Latin America's history: anarchy, caudillism, civil wars, etc. But, as Angel Rosenblat rightly says: "It is true that without any Mestizaje, the history of Spain during the last hundred and fifty years has not been more exemplary. . . ." [7] Here is another example of the pseudoscientific racism in Río de la Plata: José Ingenieros, referring to the Negroes, declared that "People of white race,

[3] Gobineau spent the years 1868–1870 as French envoy in Rio de Janeiro and was on very good terms with Emperor Pedro II. But to a friend he wrote: "This is not a country to my taste. An entirely Mulatto population, corrupted in body and soul, ugly to a terrifying degree. . . ." Gobineau (1911), 87.

[4] Sánchez (1962), 140, admits the presence of racists in Latin America but affirms: "[Racism] was not born in America but came from outside and there it has to return. . . ."

[5] Stabb (1959).

[6] Quoted by Stabb (1957), 435.

[7] J. Icaza Tijerino represents the authors trying to explain Latin American evolution racially. Rosenblat (1954), II, 185.

140

even of the inferior ethnic groups, are separated by an abyss from those beings who seem to be closer to anthropoid apes than to civilized whites. . . ." With a logic borrowed from Spencerism, the Argentine writer coldly concluded: "All that is done in favor of the inferior races is anti-scientific. At most, one might protect them so that they die out agreeably." [8]

In Chile, the triumph won in the War of the Pacific (1879–1883) was sometimes attributed to the "whiteness" of the Chileans, as compared with the "Indians" of Bolivia and Peru. Or the Chileans found consolation in the belief that mestizaje in Chile had united two "superior" races, Spaniards of the Basque-Gothic variety and the Araucanos. The assiduous historian Francisco Antonio Encina is a partisan of this naïve interpretation.[9] The serious thing about racism in Chile is that it seems to have influenced the social attitudes of the middle strata toward the lower class *rotos*, whose skin is often a shade darker.[10] In Bolivia, with its Indo-mestizo population and its tragic history, thinking along racist lines is bound to be pessimistic. In his book *Pueblo enfermo* ("A Sick People"), published in 1909, Alcides Arguedas blamed miscegenation for his country's backwardness. In Brazil, Euclides da Cunha, author of the admirable work *Os Sertões* (*Rebellion in the Backlands*) (1902), did not escape being influenced by the biological determinism of his time: "The mixture of very different races is in the majority of cases pernicious. . . . The Indo-European, the Negro, the Brazilian Guaraní or the Tapuia" represent different stages of human evolution and "the crossing, apart from obliterating the eminent qualities of the former, stimulates the revival of the primitive attributes of the latter." [11] But da Cunha was no dogmatist, and his work, above all, enhances the epic qualities displayed by men belonging to different ethnic groups during the long struggle over Canudos. Some racist intellectuals pinned their hopes on the beneficial effects of European immigration. Because of its biological superiority, the white race

[8] Quoted from a travelogue of Ingenieros, published in 1913 by Stabb (1957), 436.

[9] Griffin (1957), 26, observes, however, that: ". . . part of Encina's racism is a matter of vocabulary. Although he would be the first to deny it, much of what he interprets racially can be translated into cultural terms by the reader. . . ."

[10] Pike (1963), 36, 289–292, 444–445. He states that the Chilean middle class, "priding itself on its whiteness" are "by and large believers in the inferiority of Indians and mixed bloods."

[11] Cunha (1954), 96.

141

would impose itself on the other races. The goal was the *branquea-mento* (whitening) or *arianização*, of which Oliveira Vianna and Ellis Júnior talked.[12]

Afro-Latin Americanism

It is fascinating and even paradoxical that the intellectual environment just outlined also produced the first efforts to defend the man with dark skin and to re-evaluate his contribution and capacity. In Bolivia, it was the same Alcides Arguedas, author of *A Sick People,* who in 1919 published the first great Indianist novel, *La raza de bronce,* in which he revealed how the Indians were repressed by a rapacious clergy. Some time before the outbreak of the Mexican Revolution, in 1910, Porfirio Díaz received a proposal to set up a Mexican Indigenist Society, with the "exclusive purpose of studying our Indian races and encouraging their evolution." [13] In Brazil, Professor Nina Rodrigues of Bahia, though personally convinced of the superiority of the white race, inaugurated the dynamic and enthusiastic school of Afro-Brazilian studies. Also in Brazil, General Candido de Rondon, a convinced positivist, established in 1910 the "Serviço de Proteção aos Indios." The program of this agency, at least during its most active periods, emphasized justice and patience in dealing with the aborigines, tolerance for their religious customs, and promotion of intermarriage and trade in order to integrate the Indians with society, all of which goals are imbued with positivism. I do not know any nobler motto than that which Rondon coined for the organization — which some of its members have known how to follow: *Morrer, se preciso fôr, matar, nunca* (Die, if necessary — kill, never).[14]

The Indian peasants of Emiliano Zapata's bands, and the Plan of Ayala of 1911, written by his aide Otilio Montaño, started in Mexico the movement to give back to the Indians the lands of which they had been deprived. This aim found its legal expression in paragraph 27 of the Querétaro constitution of 1917. Interpreted in a socialist sense by President Lázaro Cárdenas, this paragraph gave rise to *ejidos,* which

[12] *IPGH* (1961), 23.
[13] Stabb (1959), 422–423; Comas (1953), 70.
[14] Kieman (1965), 263–273. The decay of the SPI became rapid and virtually boundless in recent years as disclosed by Brazilian authorities in 1968.

had more in common with modern collective farms than with the Indo-Spanish prototype. Ever since, the indígena has been present in all the numerous agrarian reform projects discussed or initiated in Latin American countries that still have "Indian" elements. In Peru, President Augusto Leguía in 1919 restored legality to the Indian communities. In Colombia, Venezuela, and Chile, there has been much discussion about the last of the Indian communities. Should they be preserved? [15] Or should they be extinguished in order to facilitate the indígena's integration with national society? The arguments for the new anti-Liberal agrarian policy obviously have been borrowed from the often anachronistic and idealized interpretations of the pre-Columbian civilizations, and also have been imported from Western socialism.[16] This was the background that created the original version of the Peruvian Aprismo of Víctor Raúl Haya de la Torre. On the other hand, Miguel Othón de Mendizábal in Mexico denied that Indian traditions dictated that the agrarian sector be collectivized as he advocated, but that economic convenience was his reason.[17] From the Marxist point of view, the Indians have deserved support mainly because they are proletarians.

In Mexico, a group of able people, idealistic and practical minded at the same time, helped intellectual indigenismo begin to express itself in social action; among them were Manuel Gamio, Moisés Sáenz, and Alfonso Caso. During the first revolutionary administrations, Indigenist policy was still experimental and vacillatory. The experiment of the so-called House of the Indian Student (*Casa del Estudiante Indígena*) reminds one of another experiment, in the sixteenth century, aimed at forming an Indian elite. In both cases, the carefully selected students, once trained in the city, failed to reintegrate with their kindred in the villages. During the Cárdenas administration, indigenist action became more vigorous. A Department of Indian Affairs was established in 1936 and work was started in the communities. In early 1940 the first Inter-American Indian Congress met in Pátzcuaro. Based primarily on Mexican experience, the recommendations of the Congress covered a

[15] Among those who have pronounced in favor of this policy are the Chilean Alejandro Lipschütz and the Colombian Juan Friede, both, incidentally, European immigrants.

[16] Salz (1944), 456.

[17] Alba (1960), 348. The Aprismo, with its eclectic ideology, started as a leftist revolutionary movement in the 1920's. Forty years later, it had become a middle-of-the-road or even right-of-middle force in Peruvian politics.

vast spectrum: study and use in education of the aboriginal languages, inalienability of the Indian communities' lands, protection of Indian handicraft, sanitation, and assistance to the indígenas in developing their gifts "so that their own culture will not disappear but serve to enrich the cultural fortune of each country. . . ." [18] As a result of the Congress, an Inter-American Indian Institute was founded. It was soon followed by various national institutes. Stimulated by this movement, indigenist legislation proliferated in the different countries, but, as during the colonial period, application often proves far more difficult. Much of positive value has been achieved, though. A visit I made to the center of the Mexican National Indian Institute in San Cristóbal Las Casas in Chiapas in 1958 impressed me very favorably.

Indigenismo as manifested in social action necessarily brings forth a crucial problem. How shall the basic aim of incorporating the indígena into modern, national society be reconciled with the desire to preserve the positive elements of the traditional culture? For Indigenistas like Gamio, the future culture of Mexico and Latin America ought to rest on a Western technological-scientific basis but should express primarily Indian-derived spiritual values.[19] But this lofty dream seems to enjoy little support and it is generally recognized that once introduced, change will necessarily affect all aspects of the Indígenas' existence, and good or bad, the process cannot be delayed for long. In the words of a Mexican specialist, Luis Mendieta y Núñez, the life of the Indígenas has to be transformed "not only from the point of view of the Indian, which is questionable, but for unquestionable reasons of national interest." [20] Such a chilly approach helps to explain a phenomenon remarked upon by anthropologist Richard Adams, who states that jungle Indians generally receive little attention from governments, for they produce little beyond subsistence, live in isolation, and do not vote.[21]

The solutions offered by modern indigenismo often are surprisingly similar to those of the Spanish colonial regime.[22] There is a risk that

[18] Ballesteros y Gaibrois and Ulloa Suárez (1961), 295. See also Comas (1964), 48–54.

[19] Alba (1960), 350–354.

[20] *Ibid.*, 356. For the Indian himself the problem can very well be as outlined by Adams (1964a), 161: "The Indian who follows his traditions is often considered a reactionary by the leftists, whereas the Indian who tries to become a Ladino may very soon be called a Communist by the Conservatives."

[21] Adams (1964b).

[22] Alba (1960), 345–346.

strengthening the Indian traditions of land tenure, and giving attention to their languages, etc., will emphasize even more the distinction between them and other citizens, which is far from desirable.[23] On the other hand, introducing accelerated change may easily lead to *Pochismo*, forming a subculture of "Lumpenproletariat." But despite all risks and dangers, the indigenistas, particularly in Mexico, have some real achievements to show. Some Indian "color" has been infused into the varied industrial civilization that is emerging today in Latin America. To give that civilization some character, some national and regional flavor, is a major task. At the same time, industrialization, if skilfully exploited, may offer new means of integrating the indígenas with national societies.

The strong links between indigenismo and some aspects of Spanish colonial policy notwithstanding, some indigenistas, or rather, those who give voice to what we may call a more romantic Indianism, have engaged in a violent struggle with the partisans of "Hispanidad." [24] In this ideological struggle, the affiliation of the former with political leftism, of the latter with political reaction, has often become apparent. Because of conflict's unyielding character, nurtured by oversimplified interpretations of the past, the cultural expressions of Indianism have sometimes become stereotyped and sterile. The same, and worse, has happened to Hispanidad.[25] Indianism therefore is in danger of becoming a road to an inverted racism. In the renowned novel by Ecuadorian Jorge Icaza, *The Huasipungo* (1934), the propagandistic message is so strong and the extreme naturalism so nauseating that the literary value suffers. On the other hand, the Peruvian Ciro Alegría, in his great work, *Wide and Alien Is the World* (1941), succeeds in presenting in a dignified and eloquent way the traditional dichotomy of the hacendado-exploiter and the Indian community fighting for its existence. The occasional Gringo "imperialist" villain in Indianist novels is a reminder that many such authors at the same time fight on the left wing of national politics. This can also, of course, be easily noticed in the works of artists such as the great Mexicans, Rivera,

[23] ". . . a romantic ideology of Indian rural existence has the paradoxical and unintended effect of hardening the caste boundaries between the Indian and the Mestizo." Kubler (1952), 65–66.

[24] Brief presentation by Diffie (1943). A more up-to-date evaluation is needed, especially on the connection between the Indian and mestizaje.

[25] For a good survey of this literature, see Zum Felde (1959), II, 254–288.

145

Orozco, and Siqueiros. Over the years, Indianism in some countries has come to be officially favored as a cultural expression, which always implies dangers for esthetic development. But, fortunately, Indianism more recently has shown symptoms of greater depth and reinterpretation, as in the works of Miguel Angel Asturias of Guatemala and José María Arguedas of Peru.[26]

The renaissance of the Indian has a weaker counterpart in the Afro-American areas, that is, in the Caribbean and Brazil. Being primarily a cultural phenomenon, its political and social implications are far less important. Since he published his first book on Cuban Negroes, the great intellectual Fernando Ortiz has been analyzing the African contribution to Caribbean society and culture. A group of Caribbean negrophiles and Negroes have created an interesting Afro-Antillean poetry.[27] In Brazil, Artur Ramos and Gilberto Freyre, the former an anthropologist, the latter a sociologist and historian, took their place in the 1930's as the principal students of the African past and present. Thanks to Freyre's efforts, the first Afro-Brazilian Congress took place in Recife in 1934. A second congress was convened in Bahia two years later. The study of the Negro's folklore and social history were emphasized. As the years passed, Freyre became increasingly idealistic in his study of racial relations in the territories colonized by the Portuguese. He has even launched "Luso-Tropicology" as a kind of special discipline or field of study.[28] Whereas the aged Freyre now emphasizes Brazilian solidarity with Portugal, the distinguished historian José Honório Rodrigues, in a recent book, stresses the bonds of common interest and friendship with the new African nations, including the nationalist rebel movement in Angola.[29]

After World War II, a research project on ethnic relations in Brazil, sponsored by UNESCO, helped to attract more attention to the social aspect. Although scholars active in the north, both North Americans and Brazilians, concluded that racial status was only one among many determinants of social class, a group of sociologists in São Paulo, led by Florestan Fernandes, seems to have reached conclusions quite unlike the view that has prevailed for more than three decades. These soci-

[26] Sommers (1964).

[27] Coulthard (1962).

[28] Stein (1961), 113, sarcastically comments: "The perfervid regionalist who once exhumed the colonial past seems now enamored of a corpse."

[29] Rodrigues (1961).

ologists, using functionalist or, in some cases, Marxist methodology, have stressed the influence exerted by prejudice in molding ethnic relations in the Brazilian south.

Meanwhile, a group of Brazilian Negro and mulatto intellectuals associated with the so-called Experimental Theater of the Negro (begun in 1944) tried to give the Negro a more active role in society instead of simply studying him. They reacted against the approach hitherto used, according to which the Negro was something exotic and alien. As one of them put it, "The Negro *is* the people in Brazil." [30] In 1950, they convoked a "Congress of the Brazilian Negro," but this "civil rights" movement seems to have collapsed, probably because of the subtlety of ethnic discrimination in Brazil.[31] Perhaps the emphasis that Freyre and others have put on "racial tolerance" in the Brazilian environment has come to overshadow socioracial problems, offering reactionary elements a welcome excuse for dismissing them as illusory.[32] But, on the other hand, an innovation such as closing ranks along more or less "racial" lines, as in the United States, would be unattractive in the Brazilian environment.

Indigenism and Afro-Latin Americanism are the ideological companions in a gigantic social change process that is bringing increasing numbers of persons of dark skin to the higher social strata. The traditional pride of lineage in the higher and middle strata seems to have weakened somewhat. Today more members of the Latin American elite are willing to say resignedly, as did Rubén Darío: "Is there a drop of blood from Africa or Chorotega or Nagrandano Indian in my veins? Perhaps there is, despite my hands of a Marquess." [33] In Castro Cuba, it seems that the profound social change that has taken place has helped to remove the traditional stigma attached to being "colored." [34] From the democratic point of view, of course, it is urgently required that similar results be obtained within a constitutional and democratic political process. Though the indígena's problem is his integration, that of the Negro and mulatto is how to fight prejudice and social degrada-

[30] Guerreiro Ramos (1957), 137.

[31] Complaints were heard at the Congress that white and mulatto leaders were taking control of the movement. Wagley (1952), 150–151.

[32] Probably one of the first foreigners to criticize this tendency of Freyre and his followers was my Swedish compatriot Prof. H. Tingsten (1950).

[33] J. Gillin in *IPGH* (1961), 13ff. Darío (1948), 187, in the foreword to *Prosas profanas* (1896).

[34] Cf. McGaffey and Barnett (1965), 337–338.

tion. This struggle, much more obvious in the United States and South Africa, seems to accompany the African presence in all multiracial environments. Whatever the nature of the problem called "racial," its solution is integrated within the construction of a more democratic society and implies making racial affiliation increasingly unimportant.

Mestizaje Reappraised

The rise of indigenismo and Africanism has had the secondary effect of bringing about a re-evaluation of mestizaje. That race mixture has no biologically negative consequences (or positive ones, for that matter) is, of course, substantiated by modern science. It is also beyond doubt that race mixture has been of enormous positive importance for Latin America in a social sense, for it has paved the way for acculturation. On the other hand, it is true that the very conditions under which miscegenation took place, the master-slave woman relationship and boundless promiscuity, gave rise to phenomena which were certainly not in keeping with the professed ethical norms. But the traditional social and sexual attitudes and the problems they engendered may well be modified by social change. Finally, as I see it, the vagueness and complexity of ethnic terminology in Latin America, produced by the general awareness there of the reality of race mixture, is a strongly positive factor. As long as this nomenclature remains complex, ethnic discrimination will be difficult to carry into effect, even though prejudice is not lacking.

In these Latin American countries, where few Indians or Negroes remain, the mestizo naturally has become a symbol of the nationality. In other countries, where these elements are still numerous, the mestizo embodies the ideal of future integration. Nevertheless, it is sometimes apparent that those who defend the mestizo take a strangely cautious position that can only be explained by the lasting effects of racist attacks against mestizaje. Luis Alberto Sánchez, for instance, declares that "The Levantine, the man of the Mediterranean, is more a hypocrite than the American Mestizo and without his excuses [!]. But nobody questions *his* traditional values and human qualities." [35] On the other hand, the word "mestizaje," which simply means "miscegenation," has become sublimated to an extreme in political rhetoric and literary prose, meaning acculturation in general or nothing concrete at

[35] Sánchez (1962), 120.

148

all. The intellectuals talk loosely about a mestizo art, a mestizo culture, or a mestizo literature. One of the present Latin American chiefs of state even used the expression "a mestizo economy" for the familiar "mixed economy." [36] If cleverly expressed, the apologetic enhancement of mestizaje values may even represent the continuation of the old Hispanidad movement to fight leftist indigenismo, because the utter sterility of pure Hispanism has become increasingly obvious. But, as already touched upon, the cult of mestizaje may also be a sincere search for a unifying formula replacing the divisive concepts of both indigenismo and Hispanidad. We wholeheartedly agree with Angel Rosenblat's observation: "The present exaltation of the Mestizo, the affirmation of a Mestizo culture or a Mestizo art imply the extension of a simple biological concept of racial character to phenomena of a complex spiritual nature. And then we fall into a kind of determinism of the blood. . . ." As this distinguished intellectual explains, as long as the mestizo was really a marginal man, in opposition to his father, it was quite natural for both literature and art to reflect this conflict. But, as soon as the population becomes more homogeneous, gradually absorbing the extremes, will not mestizaje itself dissolve? [37]

From the Latin American nationalistic point of view, it seems that Hispanidad, Africanism, indigenism, and mestizaje, as symbols, have served one and the same purpose, prolonging the historical perspective and creating links with the past that are especially required in the New World.[38] With regard to Africanism, indigenismo, and to some extent mestizaje, they help to deepen and to broaden nationalism beyond the framework established by European and Occidental civilization. But it is paradoxical that this change occurs precisely when miscegenation has become practically invisible, when acculturation is being accelerated everywhere in the far-flung region, and when the individual's racial characteristics are beginning to lose their importance in society.[39] Words like "race" and "mestizaje" are leaving their real, biological sense behind them, becoming rhetorical slogans without content. I started this book by quoting José Vasconcelos' assertion that the New World would witness the birth of a Cosmic Race; we find that whether or not this is true is completely irrelevant, as far as the mixture of

[36] Belaúnde Terry (1963).
[37] Rosenblat (1954), II, 187–188. See also Salz (1944), 469.
[38] Davis (1959), 64–65.
[39] For a contrary view, see Pitt-Rivers (1965), 47.

genes is concerned. After all, José Martí of Cuba, an older contemporary of the Mexican thinker, expressed a much more profound vision of the human reality when he wrote in 1894: "There are no races. There are only a number of variations in Man, with reference to customs and forms, imposed by the climatic and historical conditions under which he lives, which do not change that which is identical and essential. . . ." [40]

[40] Martí (1946), I, 2035. Stabb (1957); Ortiz (1945). Considering how vigorous racism was in Martí's time, his visionary intelligence is especially remarkable.

A Short Chronology

1492 Columbus' first voyage
1500 The landfall of Cabral's Portuguese expedition in Brazil
1521 Cortes' conquest of Mexico (New Spain)
1532 Pizarro's conquest of Peru
1535 New Spain becomes a viceroyalty
1542 Enactment of the "New Laws," intended to protect the Indians of Spanish America
1549 Arrival of the first Portuguese captain general and the first Jesuit missionaries in Brazil
1566 Death of Fray Bartolomé de Las Casas, "apostle of the Indians"
1580 Definitive founding of Buenos Aires (end of the era of conquest)
1609 Founding of the first Jesuit mission in Paraguay; the most famous of the Indian missions
1641 Slave hunters (*bandeirantes*) from São Paulo, Brazil, defeated by the Indians of the Spanish Jesuit missions
1654 The Dutch ousted from northeastern Brazil, which they had occupied for more than twenty years
1680 A comprehensive law book issued for Spanish America
1696 Start of the gold rush in Brazil
1713 The English take over the slave supply of Spanish America (until 1748)
1759 Expulsion of the Jesuits from the Portuguese dominions
1767 Expulsion of the Jesuits from the Spanish dominions
1780 The Indian rebellion under Tupac Amaru in Peru
1789 A Spanish slave code is issued
1804 Haiti declares itself independent
1810 Autonomous governments set up in Venezuela, Colombia, Chile, and Argentina; popular revolt in Mexico
1811 Venezuela, first Spanish American country to declare itself independent; by 1830, Mexico, Central America, Colombia, Ecuador, Peru, Bolivia, Chile, Argentina, Paraguay, and Uruguay had followed its example

151

1822	Brazil independent as an empire
1824	Battle of Ayacucho marks the end of the Spanish American wars of independence
1829	Slavery abolished in Mexico
1830	Death of Simón Bolívar, the Liberator
1847	The Maya rebellion in Yucatán, Mexico
1850	Effective measures taken by Brazil to suppress the slave trade
1851	Abolition of slavery in Colombia
1854	Abolition of slavery in Peru and Venezuela
1856	The Lerdo Law in Mexico; both Church and Indian communities are forced to sell their lands
1880	Abolition of slavery in Cuba
1888	Abolition of slavery in Brazil
1889	Fall of the Brazilian Empire
1910	Outbreak of the Mexican Revolution
1917	Enactment of the Querétaro constitution in Mexico; land reform is made a goal
1919	Legalization of the Indian communities in Peru
1940	First Inter-American Indian Congress in Pátzcuaro, Mexico
1952	The MNR (Movimiento Nacionalista Revolucionario, a more or less leftist party headed by Víctor Paz Estenssoro, recently ousted from power) revolution in Bolivia, which is followed by land reform
1959	Castro's revolution in Cuba
1961	The Alliance for Progress endorses the need for land reform in Latin America

Bibliography

Works identified by abbreviations in footnotes are fully identified here in their alphabetical places.

Acosta Saignes, Miguel
1961   "Los negros cimarrones de Venezuela," *El movimiento emancipador de Hispanoamérica: Actas y ponencias*, III. Caracas

Adams, Richard
1964a   "La mestización cultural en Centro-América," *Revista de Indias*, XXIV (Madrid)
1964b   "Politics and Social Anthropology in Spanish America," *Human Organization*, XXIII

Aguirre Beltrán, Gonzalo
1946   *La población negra de México, 1519–1810: Estudio etnohistórico.* Mexico

Aimes, H. H. S.
1908/1909   "Coartación: A Spanish Institution for the Advancement of Slaves into Freedmen," *The Yale Review*, XVII

Alba, Víctor (pseud. for Pedro Pagés)
1960   *Las ideas sociales contemporáneas en México.* Mexico

Alden, Dauril
1963   "The Population of Brazil in the Late Eighteenth Century," *The Hispanic American Historical Review*, XLIII

Allport, Gordon W.
1958   *The Nature of Prejudice.* Garden City, N.Y.

Andrade, António Alberto de
1961   *Many Races—One Nation.* Lisbon

Arcaya, Pedro M.
1949   *Insurrección de los negros de la serranía de Coro.* Caracas

Armillas, Pedro
1962   *The Native Period in the History of the New World.* Mexico (IPGH)

Arzans de Orsúa y Vela, Bartolomé
1965   *Historia de la Villa Imperial de Potosí*. Ed. with an introd.
            by Lewis Hanke and Gunnar Mendoza, I. Providence, R.I.
Ashburn, F. D. (ed.) ·
1947   *The Ranks of Death: A Medical History of the Conquest of
            America*. New York
Assunção, Fernando O.
1963   *El gaucho*. Montevideo
Azara, Félix de
1943   *Descripción e historia del Paraguay y del Río de la Plata*.
            Buenos Aires
Azevedo, Joao Lúcio de
1930   "Algumas notas relativas a pontos de história social," *Mis-
            celánea de estudos en homenagem de D. Carolina Michaelis
            de Vasconcellos*. Coimbra
Azevedo, Thales de
1961   "Italian Colonization in Southern Brazil," *Anthropological
            Quarterly*, XXXIV
Bagú, Sergio
1952   *Estructura social de la Colonia: Ensayo de historia comparada
            de América Latina*. Buenos Aires
Ballesteros y Gaibrois, Manuel and J. Ulloa Suárez
1961   *El indigenismo americano*. Madrid
Barón Castro, Rodolfo
1942   *La población de El Salvador: Estudio acerca de su desenvolvi-
            miento desde la época prehispánica hasta nuestros días*.
            Madrid
Bastide, Roger and Florestan Fernandes
1955   *Relações raciais entre negros e brancos em São Paulo*. São
            Paulo
Bastien, R.
1964   "Proceso de aculturación en las Antillas," *Revista de Indias*,
            XXIV (Madrid)
Beckman, Lars
1966   *Ras och rasfördomar*. Falköping, Sweden
Belaunde Terry, Fernando
1963   "El mestizaje de la economía," *Journal of Inter-American
            Studies*, V
Benedict, Ruth
1959   *Race: Science and Politics*. New York
Beneyto, Juan
1961   *Historia social de España y de Hispanoamérica*. Madrid
Bierck, Harold
1953   "The Struggle for Abolition in Gran Colombia," *The His-
            panic American Historical Review*, XXXIII
Bishko, C. J.
1956   "The Iberian Background of Latin American History: Recent
            Progress and Continuing Problems," *The Hispanic American
            Historical Review*, XXXVI
1952   "The Peninsular Background of Latin American Cattle
            Ranching," *The Hispanic American Historical Review*, XXXII

Blanchard, R.
1908–1910   "Les tableaux de métissage au Mexique," *Journal de la Société des Americanistes de Paris*, N.S. V, VII
Blanco, José Félix (ed.)
1875   *Documentos para la historia de la vida pública del Libertador . . .*, I. Caracas
Bolívar, Simón
1950   *Obras completas*, 2nd ed., I–III. Havana
Borah, Woodrow
1962   "América como modelo? El impacto demográfico de la expansión europea sobre el mundo no europeo," *Cuadernos Americanos*, VI
1951   *New Spain's Century of Depression*. Berkeley
1954   "Race and Class in Mexico," *Pacific Historical Review*, XXIII
———— and S. F. Cook
1962   "La despoblación del México Central en el siglo XVI," *Historia Mexicana*, XII
1966   "Marriage and Legitimacy in Mexican Culture: Mexico and California," *California Law Review*, LIV
1963   *The Aboriginal Population of Central Mexico on the Eve of the Spanish Conquest*. Berkeley
Borde, Jean and Mario Gongora
1956   *Evolución de la propiedad rural en el Valle del Puangue*, I–II. Santiago de Chile
Borges, Analola
1963   *Alvarez Abreu y su extraordinaria misión en Indias*. Santa Cruz de Tenerife
Bourne, E. G.
1962   *Spain in America, 1450–1580*. New York
Boxer, C. R.
1963   *Race Relations in the Portuguese Colonial Empire, 1415–1825*. Oxford
1962   *The Golden Age of Brazil, 1695–1750*. Berkeley
Boyd-Bowman, Peter
1963   "La emigración peninsular a América, 1520–1539," *Historia Mexicana*, XIII
Bradley, Anita
1942   *Trans-Pacific Relations of Latin America*. New York
Bray, Donald W.
1962   "The Political Emergence of Arab-Chileans, 1952–1958," *Journal of Inter-American Studies*, IV
Bremer, Fredrika
1853   *The Homes of the New World: Impressions of America*, I–III. London.
Brito Figueroa, Federico
1960   *Ensayos de historia social venezolana*. Caracas
1963   *La estructura económica de Venezuela colonial*. Caracas
Buarque de Holanda, Sérgio (ed.)
1960   *História geral da civilização brasileira*, I:I-II. São Paulo
1956   *Raízes do Brasil*, 3rd ed. Rio de Janeiro

Bueno, Cosme
1951   Geografía del Perú virreinal (siglo XVIII). Ed. by D. Valcar-
               cel. Lima
Bushnell, David
1954   The Santander Regime in Gran Colombia. Newark, Del.
Calmon, Pedro
1937   História social do Brasil, 4th ed., I. São Paulo
Cardoso, Fernando Henrique
1962   Capitalismo e escravidão no Brazil Meridional. São Paulo
———— and Octavio Ianni
1960   Côr e mobilidade social em Florianópolis. São Paulo
Cardozo, Efraín
1959   El Paraguay colonial. Buenos Aires
Cardozo, Manoel
1960/1961   "Slavery in Brazil as Described by Americans, 1822–1888,"
               The Americas, XVII
Carmagnani, Marcelo
1963   El salariado minero en Chile colonial: su desarrollo en una
               sociedad provincial: El Norte Chico, 1690–1800. Santiago
———— and Herbert S. Klein
1965   "Demografía histórica: La población del Obispado de Santi-
               ago, 1777–1778," Boletin de la Academia Chilena de His-
               toria, XXXII
Carneiro, Edison
1964   Ladinos e crioulos: Estudos sôbre o negro no Brasil. Rio de
               Janeiro
1958   O Quilombo dos Palmares, 2nd ed. São Paulo
Carneiro de Mendonça, Marcos
1963   A Amazonia na era pombalina, II–III. São Paulo
1960   O Marquês de Pombal e o Brasil. São Paulo
Carrera Damas, Germán
1964   Sobre el significado socioeconómico de la acción histórica de
               Boves. Caracas
Carrera Stampa, Manuel
1954   Los gremios mexicanos. Mexico
Cartas de Indias. Madrid 1877
Carvalho Neto, Paulo de
1962   "Antología del negro paraguayo," Anales de la Universidad
               Central, XCI (Quito)
Catálogo   Catálogo de pasajeros a Indias durante los siglos XVI, XVII
               y XVIII, I–III. Seville 1940–1946
(CDFS)   Colección de documentos para la formación social de His-
               panoamérica, 1493–1810, I–III:2 (Madrid 1953–1962)
(CDIHCh)   Colección de documentos inéditos para la historia de Chile.
               Ed. by J. T. Medina, 2nd series, III. Santiago 1959
Cervantes Saavedra, Niguel de
1949   Obras completas. Ed. by A. Valbuena Prat. Madrid
Chamberlin, Taylor
1966   The Formation of a Native Clergy in Colonial Spanish Amer-
               ica. Unpublished M.A. thesis, Columbia University
Chang-Rodríguez, Eugenio
1958   "Chinese Labor Migration into Latin America in the Nine-

teenth Century," *Revista de Historia de América*, XLVI (Mexico)

Chávez, Ezequiel A.
1957   *Morelos*. Mexico

Chávez Orozco, Luis
1938   *Historia económica y social de México*. Mexico
1943   *Las instituciones democráticas de los indígenas mexicanos en la época colonial*. Mexico

Chevalier, François
1956   *La formación de los grandes latifundios en México*. Mexico (Problemas agrícolas e industriales de Mexico). The American edition unfortunately lacks the scholarly apparatus.

Cieza de León, Pedro de
1881   *Guerras civiles del Perú: II. Guerra de Chupas*. Madrid (Colección de documentos inéditos para la historia de España. LXXVII.)
1945   *La crónica del Perú*. Buenos Aires

Coll y Prat, Narciso
1960   *Memoriales sobre la Independencia de Venezuela*. Madrid (Biblioteca de la Academia Nacional de la Historia, Venezuela, XXIII)

Columbus, Christopher
1961   *Four Voyages to the New World: Letters and Selected Documents*. New York
1960   *The Journal of Christopher Columbus*. Transl. by C. Jane with an appendix by R. A. Skelton. New York

Comas, Juan
1944   "El mestizaje y su importancia social," *Acta Americana*, II (Austin, Tex.)
1953   *Ensayos sobre el indigenismo*. Mexico
1964   *La antropología social aplicada en México: Trayectoria y antología*. Mexico

"Concolorcorvo" (pseud.)
1942   *El Lazarillo de ciegos caminantes desde Buenos Aires a Lima (1773)*. Buenos Aires

Coni, Emilio A.
1945   *El gaucho: Argentina — Brasil — Uruguay*. Buenos Aires

Conrad, Alfred H. and John R. Meyer
1964   *The Economics of Slavery and Other Studies in Econometric History*. Chicago

Cook, S. F. and W. Borah
1963   "Quelle fut la stratification sociale au Centre du Mexique pendant la première moitié du XVIᵉ siècle?", *Anales: Économies, sociétés, civilisations*, XVIII
1960   *The Indian Population of Central Mexico, 1531–1610*. Berkeley

——— and L. B. Simpson
1948   *The Population of Mexico in the Sixteenth Century*. Berkeley

Córdoba, Matías de
1937   "Utilidades de que todos los indios y ladinos se vistan y calcen a la española (1797)," *Anales de la Sociedad de Geografía e Historia*, XIV (Guatemala)

Corominas, J.
1954   Diccionario crítico etimológico de la lengua castellana, I.
              Madrid
Correia Lopes, Edmundo
1944   A escravatura: Subsídios para a sua história. Lisbon
Cortés, Vicenta
1964   La esclavitud en Valencia durante el reinado de los Reyes
              Católicos (1479–1516). Valencia
Cortés y Larraz, Pedro
1958   Descripción geográfico-moral de la diócesis de Goathemala
              . . . , I–II. Guatemala
Costales, Piedad de P.
1962   "El huasipungo y su evolución histórica," Anales de la Uni-
              versidad Central, XCI (Quito)
Coulthard, G. R.
1962   Race and Colour in Caribbean Literature. London and New
              York
Cumberland, Charles C.
1960   "The Sonora Chinese and the Mexican Revolution," The
              Hispanic American Historical Review, XL
Cunha, Euclides da
1954   Os Sertões (Campanha de Canudos), 23rd ed. Rio de Ja-
              neiro
Dahl, Victor C.
1960/1961   "Alien Labor on the Gulf of Mexico, 1880–1900," The
              Americas, XVII
Darío, Rubén
1948   Obras completas. Buenos Aires
Davidson, Basil
1961   Black Mother, Africa: The Years of Trial. London
Davidson, David M.
1966   "Negro Slave Control and Resistance in Colonial Mexico,
              1519–1650," The Hispanic American Historical Review,
              XLVI
Davis, David Brion
1966   The Problem of Slavery in Western Culture. Ithaca, N.Y.
Davis, Harold E.
1959   "Trends in Social Thought in Twentieth Century Latin
              America," Journal of Inter-American Studies, I
Depons, Francisco
1960   Viaje a la parte oriental de Tierra Firme en la América Meri-
              dional, I–II. Caracas
Dessaint, Alain Y.
1962   "Effects of the Hacienda and Plantation Systems on Guate-
              mala's Indians," América Indígena, XXII (Mex   )
Díaz del Castillo, Bernal
1955   Historia verdadera de la conquista de la Nueva   .paña, I–II.
              Mexico
Díaz Soler, L. M.
1953   Historia de la esclavitud negra en Puerto Rico, 1493–1890.
              Madrid

158

Diffie, Bailey W.
1945   *Latin American Civilization: Colonial Period.* Harrisburg, Pa.
1943   "The Ideology of Hispanidad," *The Hispanic American Historical Review*, XXIII
Dobyns, Henry F.
1963   "An Outline of Andean Epidemic History to 1720," *Bulletin of the History of Medicine*, XXXVII
Domínguez Ortiz, Antonio
1952   "La esclavitud en Castilla durante la edad moderna," *Estudios de Historia Social de España*, II (Madrid)
Dunn, L. C. and T. Dobzhansky
1952   *Heredity, Race and Society.* New York
Elkins, Stanley M.
1959   *Slavery.* Chicago
Endrek, Emiliano
1966   *El mestizaje en Córdoba: Siglo XVIII y principios del XIX.* Córdoba, Argentina
(*Epistolario*)   *Epistolario de la Primera República*, II. Caracas 1960
Fals Borda, Orlando
1957   *El hombre y la tierra en Boyacá: Bases sociológicas e históricas para una reforma agraria.* Bogotá
Felice Cardot, Carlos
1952   *La rebelión de Andresote (Valles de Yaracuay, 1730–1733).* Caracas
Feliú Cruz, Guillermo
1942   *La abolición de la esclavitud en Chile.* Santiago
Fernandes, Florestan
1965   *A integração do negro á sociedade de clases.* I-II. São Paulo
Flores Moncayo, José (ed.)
1953   *Legislación boliviana del indio.* La Paz
Franco, José L.
1961   *Afroamérica.* Havana
Frazier, Franklin
1957   *Race and Culture Contacts in the Modern World.* New York
Freyre, Gilberto
1950   *Casa Grande e Senzala: Formação da família brasileira sob o regime de economia patriarcal*, 6th ed., I–II. Rio de Janeiro
1963a   *New World in the Tropics.* New York
1963b   *O escravo nos anúncios de jornais brasileiros do século XIX: Tentativa de interpretação antropológica, através de anúncios de jornais, de característicos de personalidade e de deformação de corpo de negros. . . .* Recife
1959   *Ordem e progresso: Processo de desintegração das sociedades patriarcal e semipatriarcal no Brasil sob o regime de trabalho livre . . .* , I–II. Rio de Janeiro
1951   *Sobrados e mucambos: Decadencia do patriacado rural e desenvolvimento do urbano*, 2nd ed., I–III. Rio de Janeiro and São Paulo
Friede, Juan
1952   "Algunas observaciones sobre la realidad de la emigración espanola a América en la primera mitad del siglo XVI," *Revista de Indias*, XII (Madrid)

1963a	"El factor demográfico en la conquista de América," *Banco de, la República: Biblioteca Luis Ángel Arango. Boletín Cultural y Bibliográfico*, VI (Bogotá)
1944	*El indio en la lucha por la tierra: Historia de los resguardos del Macizo Central Colombiano.* Bogotá
1965	"La extraordinaria experiencia de Francisco Martín (1531–1533)," *Fundación John Boulton. Boletín Histórico*, no. 7 (Caracas)
1963b	*Los quimbayas bajo la dominación española: Estudio documental.* Bogotá
1961	*Los Welser en la conquista de Venezuela.* Caracas
1951	"The Catálogo de Pasajeros and Spanish Emigration to America to 1550," *The Hispanic American Historical Review*, XXXI

Furtado, Celso
1959	*Formação econômica do Brasil.* Rio de Janeiro

Garzón Maceda, Ceferino and José Walter Dorflinger
1961	"Esclavos y mulatos en un dominio rural del siglo XVIII en Córdoba: Contribución a la demografía histórica," *Revista de la Universidad Nacional de Córdoba*, II (Córdoba, Argentina)

Gibson, Charles
1964	*The Aztecs Under Spanish Rule: A History of the Indians of the Valley of Mexico, 1519–1810.* Stanford, Calif.
1954	"The Transformation of the Indian Community in New Spain, 1500–1810," *Cahiers d'Histoire Mondiale*, II (Paris)

Gilmore, Robert L.
1964	*Caudillism and Militarism in Venezuela, 1810–1910.* Athens, Ohio

Gobineau, Joseph Arthur de
1911	*Nachgelassene Schriften des Grafen Gobineau herausgegeben von L. Schemann: Briefe . . . mit A. v. Keller.* Strassburg

Góngora, Bartolomé de
1960	*El Corregidor Sagaz.* Madrid

Góngora, Mario
1951	*El estado en el derecho indiano: Época de fundación, 1492–1570.* Santiago de Chile
1962	*Los grupos de conquistadores en Tierra Firme (1509–1530): Fisonomía histórico-social de un tipo de conquista.* Santiago de Chile
1960	*Origen de los inquilinos en Chile Central.* Santiago
1965	"Regimen señorial y rural en la Extremadura de la Orden de Santiago en el momento de la emigración a Indias," *Jahrbuch für Geschichte von Staat, Wirtschaft und Gesellschaft Lateinamerikas*, II (Cologne)
1966	"Vagabondage et société pastorale en Amérique Latine (spécialement au Chili Central)," *Annales: Sociétés, economies, civilisations*, XXI (Paris)

González del Cossío, F. (ed.)
1958	*Legislación indigenista de México: Recopilación.* Mexico (Instituto Indigenista Interamericano)

160

González Navarro, Moisés
1955   "La política social de Hidalgo," *Anales del Instituto Nacional de Antropología e Historia*, 1953, VII: 36 (Mexico)
1957   *La vida social: Mexico* (in D. Cosío Villegas, *Historia moderna de México: El Porfiriato*)
Gouveia, Elsa
1960   "The West India Slave Laws of the Eighteenth Century," *Revista de Ciencias Sociales*, IV (Rio Piedras, P.R.)
Graaner, J. A.
1949   *Las provincias del Río de la Plata en 1816.* Buenos Aires
Graham, Richard
1966   "Causes for the Abolition of Negro Slavery in Brazil: An Interpretive Essay," *The Hispanic American Historical Review*, XLVI
Greenleaf, R. E.
1965   "The Inquisition and the Indians of New Spain: A Study in Jurisdictional Confusion," *The Americas*, XXII
Griffin, Charles
1957   "Francisco Encina and Revisionism in Chilean History," *The Hispanic American Historical Review*, XXXVII
1962   *Los temas sociales y económicos en la época de la Independencia.* Caracas
Guerreiro Ramos, A.
1957   *Introdução crítica à sociologia brasileira.* Rio de Janeiro
Guillot, Carlos Federico
1961   *Negros rebeldes y negros cimarrones: Perfil afroamericano en la historia del Nuevo Mundo durante el siglo XVI.* Buenos Aires
Gumilla, José
n.d.   *El Orinoco Ilustrado* (1740). Ed. by C. Bayle. Madrid
Guthrie, Chester L.
1945   "Riots in Seventeenth Century Mexico City: A Study of Social and Economic Conditions," *Greater America: Essays in Honor of H. Bolton.* Berkeley
Gutiérrez de Pineda, Virginia
1963   *La familia en Colombia*, I. Bogotá
Haring, C. H.
1963   *The Spanish Empire in America.* New York
Harris, Marvin
1964   *Patterns of Race in the Americas.* New York
Harth-terré, Emilio
n.d.   *Ponencia presentada al III Congreso Nacional de Historia Peruana.* Multigr.
1961   "El esclavo negro en la sociedad indoperuana," *Journal of Inter-American Studies*, III
———— and Alberto Márquez-Abanto
1962   "Perspectiva social y económica del artesano virreinal en Lima," *Revista del Archivo Nacional del Perú*, XXVI
Hartz, Louis (ed.)
1964   *The Founding of New Societies.* New York

Henao, Jesús M. and Gerardo Arrubla
1938   *History of Colombia.* Transl. Chapel Hill, N.C.
(*HDM*)   *Historia documental de México,* I–II. Mexico 1964
Hoetink, Harry
1961   "Colonial Psychology and Race," *Journal of Economic History,* XXI
(*HSAI*)   *Handbook of South American Indians,* II. Washington, D.C. 1946
Hudson, Randall O.
1964   "The Status of the Negro in Northern South America, 1820–1860," *The Journal of Negro History,* XLIX
Humboldt, Alexander von
1941   *Ensayo político sobre el reino de la Nueva España,* 6th ed., II. Mexico
1956   *Viaje a las regiones equinocciales del nuevo continente . . . ,* I–V. Caracas
Humphreys, R. A.
1946   *Modern Latin America.* London
Hutchinson, Henry William
1957   *Village and Plantation Life in Northeastern Brazil.* Seattle
Ianni, Octávio
1962   *As metamorfoses do escravo: apogeu e crise da escravatura no Brasil Meridional.* São Paulo
(ILO 1953)   *Indigenous Peoples: Living and Working Conditions of Aboriginal Populations in Independent Countries.* Geneva 1953. (International Labour Office)
(ILO 1957)   *The Landless Farmer in Latin America.* Geneva 1957 (International Labour Office)
(*Instruciones*)   *Instruciones que los Vireyes de Nueva España dejaron a sus sucesores,* II. Mexico 1873
(IPGH)   *El mestizaje en la historia de Ibero-América.* Mexico 1961 (Instituto Panamericano de Geografía e Historia)
Irie, Toraji
1951–1952   "History of Japanese Migration to Peru," *The Hispanic American Historical Review,* XXXI–XXXII
Iturriaga, José
1951   *La estructura social y cultural de México.* Mexico and Buenos Aires
James, Preston E.
1950   *Latin America,* Rev. ed. New York
Jara, Alvaro
1959   *Los asientos de trabajo y la provisión de mano de obra para los no-encomenderos en la ciudad de Santiago, 1586–1600.* Santiago de Chile
——— (ed.)
1956   *Legislación indigenista de Chile.* Mexico (Instituto Indigenista Interamericano)
Jaramillo Uribe, Jaime
1963   "Esclavos y señores en la sociedad colombiana del siglo XVIII," *Anuario Colombiano de Historia Social y de la Cultura,* I: I (Bogotá)

1964   "La población indígena de Colombia en el momento de la Conquista y sus transformaciones posteriores," *Anuario Colombiano de Historia Social y de la Cultura*, I: II (Bogotá)

Jiménez Pastrana, Juan
1963   *Los chinos en las luchas por la Liberación Cubana, 1847–1930.* Havana

Juan, Jorge and Antonio de Ulloa
1768   *A Voyage to South America . . . ,* I–II. London
1953   *Noticias secretas de América.* Buenos Aires

Kiemen, Mathias
1965   "The Status of the Indian in Brazil after 1820," *The Americas*, XXI

King, James F.
1953a   "A Royalist View of the Colored Castes in the Venezuelan War of Independence," *The Hispanic American Historical Review*, XXXIII
1943   "Descriptive Data on Negro Slaves in Spanish Importation Records and Bills of Sale," *The Journal of Negro History*, XXVIII
1945   "Negro Slavery in New Granada," *Greater America: Essays in Honor of H. E. Bolton.* Berkeley
1951   "The Case of José Ponciano de Ayarza: A Document on Gracias al Sacar," *The Hispanic American Historical Review*, XXXI
1953b   "The Colored Castes and American Representation in the Cortes of Cadiz," *The Hispanic American Historical Review*, XXXIII
1942   "The Evolution of the Free Slave Trade Principle in Spanish Colonial Administration," *The Hispanic American Historical Review*, XXII
1944   "The Latin American Republics and the Suppression of the Slave Trade," *The Hispanic American Historical Review*, XXIV

Klein, Herbert S.
1966   "Anglicanism, Catholicism, and the Negro Slave," *Comparative Studies in Society and History*, VIII. Includes comment by E. Gouveia

Konetzke, Richard
1965   *Die Indianerkulturen Altamerikas und die Spanisch-Portugiesische Kolonialherrschaft.* Frankfurt am Main (Fischer Weltgeschichte, 22.)
1946a   "Documentos para la historia y crítica de los registros parroquiales en las Indias," *Revista de Indias*, VII (Madrid)
1946b   "El mestizaje y su importancia en el desarrollo de la población hispanoamericana durante la época colonial," *Revista de Indias*, VII (Madrid)
1951a   "Estado y sociedad en las Indias," *Estudios Americanos*, III (Seville)
1945   "La emigración de mujeres españolas a América durante la época colonial," *Revista Internacional de Sociología*, III (Madrid)

163

1952   "La emigración española al Río de la Plata durante el siglo
                XVI," *Miscelánea Americanista* (*Homenaje a D. Antonio
                Ballesteros Beretta*), III. Madrid
1949a   "La esclavitud de los indios como elemento de la estructu-
                ración social de Hispanoamérica," *Estudios de Historia Social
                de España*, I (Madrid)
1951b   "La formación de la nobleza en Indias," *Anuario de Estudios
                Americanos*, III (Seville)
1948   "Las fuentes para la historia demográfica de Hispanoamérica
                durante la época colonial," *Anuario de Estudios Americanos*,
                V (Seville)
1949b   "Las ordenanzas de gremios como documentos para la his-
                toria social de Hispanoamérica durante la época colonial,"
                Estudios de Historia Social de España, I (Madrid)
1960   "Los mestizos en la legislación colonial," *Revista de Estudios
                Políticos*, 112 (Madrid)

Kroeber, A. L.
1939   *Cultural and Natural Areas of Native South America*. Berkeley
Kubler, George
1952   *The Indian Caste of Peru, 1795–1940: A Population Study
                Based upon Tax Records and Census Reports*. Washington,
                D.C.
Lafuente Machain, R. de
1939   *El gobernador Domingo Martínez de Irala*. Buenos Aires
Lanning, John T.
1955   *The University in the Kingdom of Guatemala*. Ithaca, N.Y.
Leal, Ildefonso
1963   *Historia de la Universidad de Caracas (1721–1827)*. Caracas
Lecuna, Vicente
1956   *Catálogo de errores y calumnias en la historia de Bolívar*, I,
                New York
——— (ed.)
1929–   *Cartas del Libertador*, I–VI. Caracas
León, Nicolás
1924   *La castas del México colonial o Nueva España*. Mexico
Levillier, Roberto (ed.)
1922   *Audiencia de Lima: Correspondencia de presidentes y oidores*,
                I. Madrid
Lewín, Boleslao
1943   *Tupac Amaru, el rebelde, su época, sus luchas y su influencia
                en el continente*. Buenos Aires
Lier, Rudolf van
1949   *Samenleving in een grensgebied: Een sociaal-historische studie
                van de maatschappij in Suriname*. The Hague
(LIP)   *Legislación indigenista del Perú*. Lima 1948 (Dirección gen-
                eral de asuntos indígenas)
Lipschütz, Alejandro
1944   *El indoamericanismo y el problema racial en las Américas*,
                2nd ed. Santiago de Chile
Lissón Chávez, Emilio (ed.)
1943–1956   *La Iglesia de España en el Perú: Colección de documentos
                para la historia . . .*, 1–25. Seville

164

Lombardi, John V.
1967   "Los esclavos en la legislación republicana de Venezuela,"
            Fundación John Boulton. Boletín Histórico, no. 13 (Caracas)
López Martínez, Héctor
1965   "Un motín de mestizos en el Perú (1567)," Revista de
            Indias, XXIV (Madrid)
López Sarrelangue, D. E.
1962   "Población indígena de la Nueva España en el siglo XVIII,"
            Historia Mexicana, XII
McAlister, Lyle N.
1957   El Fuero Militar in New Spain, 1764–1800. Gainesville, Fla.
1963   "Social Structure and Social Change in New Spain," The
            Hispanic American Historical Review, XLIII
MacGaffey, Wyatt and Clifford R. Barnett
1965   Twentieth-Century Cuba: The Background of the Castro
            Revolution. Garden City, N.Y.
Machado, José de Alcântara
1953   Vida e morte do bandeirante. São Paulo
Machado Filho, Aires da Mata
1943   O negro e o garimpo em Minas Gerais. Rio de Janeiro
Madariaga, Salvador de
1952   Bolívar. London
Malagón, Javier
1956   "Un documento del siglo XVIII para la historia de la esclavi-
            tud en las Antillas," Miscelánea de estudios dedicados a
            Fernando Ortiz, II. Havana
Maldonado de Guevara, Francisco
1924   El primer contacto de blancos y gentes de color en América:
            Estudio sobre el diario del primer viaje de Cristóbal Colón.
            Valladolid
Manzoni, C.
1939   El indio en la poesía de América española. Buenos Aires
Marshall, C. E.
1939   "The Birth of the Mestizo in New Spain," The Hispanic
            American Historical Review, XIX
Martí, José
1946   Obras completas, I. Havana
Martin, Norman F.
1957   Los vagabundos en la Nueva España: Siglo XVI. Mexico
Masini, José Luis
1962   La esclavitud negra en Mendoza: época independiente. Men-
            doza, Argentina
Massini Ezcurra, José M.
1961   "Redhibitoria y esclavos en el Río de la Plata," Archivo
            Iberoamericano de Historia de la Medicina y Antropología
            Médica, XIII (Buenos Aires)
Masur, Gerhard
1948   Simón Bolívar. Albuquerque, N.M.
Mauro, Frédéric
1960   Le Portugal et l'Atlantique au XVIIe siècle (1570–1670).
            Paris

Mayer, Kurt B.
1955   *Class and Society.* New York
Means, P. A.
1931   *Ancient Civilizations of the Andes.* London
Medina, José Toribio
1952   *Historia del Tribunal del Santo Oficio de la Inquisición en Chile.* Santiago
Meléndez, Concha
1934   *La novela indianista en la América hispana, 1832–1889.* Madrid
Mellafe, Rolando
1964   *La esclavitud en Hispanoamérica.* Buenos Aires
1959   *La introducción de la esclavitud negra en Chile: Tráfico y rutas.* Santiago
(Memorias)   *Memorias de los Vireyes que han gobernado el Perú,* I. Lima 1859
(Métodos)   *Métodos y resultados de la política indigenista en México.* Mexico 1954 (Memorias del Instituto Nacional Indigenista, VI)
Mintz, Sidney
1959   "Labor and Sugar in Jamaica and Puerto Rico, 1800–1850," *Comparative Studies in Society and History,* I (The Hague)
1951   "The Role of Forced Labour in Nineteenth Century Puerto Rico," *Caribbean Historical Review,* II
Miranda, Francisco de
1950   *Archivo del General Miranda,* XXI–XXII (Havana)
Miranda, José
1962   "La población indígena de México en el siglo XVII," *Historia Mexicana,* XII
1964   "Los indígenas de América en la época colonial: teorías, legislación, realidades," *Cuadernos Americanos,* XXIII (Mexico)
Molina, Pedro
1954   *Escritos,* III. Guatemala
Mora, María José Luis
1963   *Obras sueltas,* 2nd ed. Mexico
Mörner, Magnus
1964a   "Das Verbot für die Encomenderos unter ihren eigenen Indianern zu wohnen," *Jahrbuch für Geschichte von Staat, Wirtschaft und Gesellschaft Lateinamerikas,* I (Cologne)
1965b   "En torno a la penetración mestiza en los pueblos de indios, las composiciones de tierras y los encomenderos en el Perú en el siglo XVII," *Revista Histórica,* XXVIII (Lima)
1960   "Invandringen och det moderna Latinamerikas tillblivelse," *Ymer* (Stockholm, Sweden)
1962   "La afortunada gestión de un misionero del Perú en Madrid en 1578," *Anuario de Estudios Americanos,* XIX (Seville)
1967   "La difusión del castellano y el aislamiento de los indios — dos aspiraciones contradictorias de la Corona española," *Homenaje a Jaime Vicens Vives,* II (Barcelona)
1966a   "La infiltración mestiza en los cacicazgos y cabildos de indios (siglos XVI–XVIII)," *XXXVI Congreso Internacional de Americanistas, España, 1964: Actas y Memorias,* II (Seville)
1964b   "La política de segregación y el mestizaje en la Audiencia de Guatemala," *Revista de Indias,* XXIV (Madrid)

1963   "Las comunidades de indígenas y la legislación segregacionista en el Nuevo Reino de Granada," *Anuario Colombiano de Historia Social y de la Cultura*, I: I (Bogotá)

1966b   "Los esfuerzos realizados por la Corona para separar negros e indios en Hispanoamérica durante el siglo XVI," *Homenaje. Estudios de filología e historia literaria lusohispanas e iberoamericanas publicados para celebrar el tercer lustro del Instituto de Estudios Hispánicos, Portugueses e Iberoamericanos de la Universidad Estatal de Utrecht.* The Hague

1964c   "Race and Class in Twentieth Century Latin America," *Cahiers d'Histoire Mondiale*, VIII (Paris)

1965   "Separación o integración? En torno al debate dieciochesco sobre los principios de la política indigenista en Hispano-América," *Journal de la Société des Américanistes*, LIV: I (Paris)

1961a   "Teoría y práctica de la segregación racial en la América colonial española," *Boletín de la Academia Nacional de la Historia*, XLIV (Caracas)

1961b   "The Guaraní Missions and the Segregation Policy of the Spanish Crown," *Archivum Historicum Societatis Iesu*, XXX (Rome)

1966c   "The History of Race Relations in Latin America: Some Comments on the State of Research," *Latin American Research Review*, I: 3

———— and Charles Gibson

1962   "Diego Muñoz Camargo and the Segregation Policy of the Spanish Crown," *The Hispanic American Historical Review*, XLII

Morse, Richard

1958   *From Community to Metropolis: A Biography of São Paulo, Brazil.* Gainesville, Fla.

1964   "Negro-White Relations in Latin America," *Reports and Speeches of the Ninth Yale Conference on the Teaching of Social Sciences.* New Haven, Conn. Multigr.

Mosk, Sanford A.

1948   "Latin America and the World Economy, 1850–1914," *Inter-American Economic Affairs*, II

Muguburu, J. and F. de

1928   *Diario de Lima* (*1640–1649*), I. Lima

Nóbrega, Manoel da

1955   *Cartas do Brasil e mais escritos . . . com introdução e notas históricas e críticas de S. Leite.* Coimbra

Ornellas, Manoelito de

1956   *Gaúchos e beduínos: A origem étnica e a formação social do Rio Grande do Sul*, 2nd ed. Rio de Janeiro

Ortiz, Fernando

1916   *Hampa afro-cubana. Los negros esclavos. . . .* Havana

1945   "Martí y las razas de librería," *Cuadernos Americanos*, XXI (Mexico)

Ospina Perez, Luis

1955   *Industria y protección en Colombia 1810–1930.* Medellín

Othón de Mendizabal, Miguel
1946   *Obras completas*, IV. Mexico
Ots Capdequí, J. M.
1957   *El estado español en las Indias*, 3rd ed. Buenos Aires and
                Mexico
1958   *Las instituciones del Nuevo Reino de Granada al tiempo de
                la Independencia*. Madrid
Otte, Enrique and Conchita Ruíz-Burruecos
1963   "Los portugueses en la trata de esclavos negros en las postri-
                merías del siglo XVI," *Moneda y Crédito*, LXXXV (Ma-
                drid)
Ovalle, Alonso de
1888   "Histórica Relación del Reino de Chile," *Colección de His-
                toriadores Chilenos*, XII. Santiago
Oviedo, Basilio Vicente de
1930   *Cualidades y riquezas del Nuevo Reino de Granada*. Bogotá
Palacios de la Vega, Joseph
1955   *Diario de viaje entre los indios y negros de la Provincia de
                Cartagena en el Nuevo Reino de Granada, 1787–1788*. Ed.
                by G. Reichel-Dolmatoff. Bogotá
(PAU 1959)   *Plantation Systems of the New World*. Washington, D.C.
                (Pan American Union)
Paz, Octavio
1950   *El laberinto de la soledad*. Mexico
(*Pensamiento*) *El pensamiento constitucional hispanoamericano hasta 1830:
                Compilación de constituciones sancionadas y proyectos con-
                stitucionales*, V. Caracas 1961
Pereda Valdés, Ildefonso
1941   *Negros esclavos y negros libres*. Montevideo.
Pérez, Aquiles R.
1947   *Las mitas en la Real Audiencia de Quito*. Quito
Pérez Barradas, José
1948   *Los mestizos de América*. Madrid
Pérez de Tudela Bueso, José
1960   "Ideario de Don Francisco Rodríguez, párroco criollo en los
                Andes," *Anuario de Estudios Americanos*, XVII (Seville)
Petit Muñoz, E., E. Narancio, and J. M. Traibel Nelcis
1947   *La condición jurídica, social, económica y política de los
                negros durante el coloniaje en la Banda Oriental*, I. Monte-
                video
Picón-Salas, Mariano
1963   *A Cultural History of Spanish America: From the Conquest
                to Independence*. Berkeley
Pike, Fredrick
1963   *Chile and the United States: The Emergence of Chile's Social
                Crisis and the Challenge to United States Diplomacy*. South
                Bend, Ind.
Pitt-Rivers, Julian
1965   "Who are the Indians?", *Encounter*, XXV: 3 (London)
Polo, J. T. (ed.)
1899   *Memorias de los virreyes del Perú: Marqués de Mancera y
                Conde de Salvatierra*. Lima

Poma de Ayala, Phelipe Guamán
1944   *Primer Nueva Coronica y Buen Gobierno.* Ed. by A. Posnan-
               sky. La Paz
Posada, Germán
1963   "La idea de América en Vasconcelos," *Historia Mexicana,*
               XII
Prado Junior, Caio
1961   *Formação do Brasil contemporâneo: Colônia,* 6th ed. São
               Paulo
Priestley, Herbert I.
1929   *The Coming of the White Man, 1492–1848.* New York
Rama, Carlos
1957   "Os movimentos sociais na América Latina durante o século
               XIX," *Revista de História,* VIII: 30 (São Paulo)
(RI)   *Recopilación de Leyes de los Reinos de las Indias.* Madrid
               1680
Redfield, Robert
1941   *The Folk Culture of Yucatán.* Chicago
Reed, Nelson
1964   *The Caste War of Yucatán.* Stanford, Calif.
Reyes Heroles, Jesús
1961   *Liberalismo mexicano.* I–III. Mexico
Ricardo, Cassiano
1942   *Marcha para Oeste: A influencia da bandeira na formação
               social e política do Brasil,* 2nd ed., I–II. Rio de Janeiro
Roche, Jean
1959   *La colonisation allemande et le Rio Grande do Sul.* Paris
Rodrigues, José Honório
1961   *Brasil e a Africa: outro horizonte.* Rio de Janeiro
Rodríguez Molas, Ricardo
1964   "El gaucho rioplatense: origen, desarrollo y marginalidad so-
               cial," *Journal of Inter-American Studies,* IV
1961   "Los negros libres rioplatenses," *Buenos Aires. Revista de
               Humanidades,* I
Romero, Carlos Alberto (ed.)
1901   *Memoria del Virrey del Perú Marqués de Avilés.* Lima
Romero, Emilio
1949   *Historia económica del Perú.* Buenos Aires
Romero, Fernando
1942   "José Manuel Valdés, Great Peruvian Mulatto," *Phylon,* III
Roncal, Joaquín
1944   "The Negro Race in Mexico," *The Hispanic American His-
               torical Review,* XXIV
Rosenblat, Angel
1945   *La población indígena de América desde 1492 hasta la actual-
               idad.* Buenos Aires
1954   *La población indígena y el mestizaje en América,* I–II. Buenos
               Aires. New ed. of the preceding item.
Roys, Ralph
1943   *The Indian Background of Colonial Yucatán.* Washington,
               D.C.

Rubio Orbe, Alfredo (ed.)
1954   *Legislación indigenista del Ecuador.* Mexico (Instituto Indigenista Interamericano)
Ruíz, Hipólito
1952   *Relación histórica del viage que hizo a los Reynos del Perú y Chile . . . en el año 1777 hasta el de 1788,* I–II. Madrid
Rumazo Gonzalez, J. (ed.)
1934   *Libro segundo de Cabildos de Quito,* II. Quito
Sacchetti, Alfredo
1964   "Capacidad respiratoria y aclimatación en las razas andinas," *Journal de la Société des Américanistes,* LIII (Paris)
Saco, José Antonio
1938   *Historia de la esclavitud de la raza africana en el Nuevo Mundo y en especial en los países américo-hispanos,* I–IV. Havana
Sáenz, Moisés
1933   *Sobre el indio peruano y su incorporación al medio nacional.* Mexico
Saito, Hiroshi
1961   *O japones no Brasil.* São Paulo
Salas, Alberto M.
1960   *Crónica florida del mestizaje de las Indias: Siglo XVI.* Buenos Aires
Saldanha, P. E.
1964   "Aspectos demográficos y genéticos del mestizaje en América del Sur," *Revista de Indias,* XXIV (Madrid)
Salz, Beate
1944   "Indianismo," *Social Research,* XI
Sánchez, Luis Alberto
1962   *Examen espectral de América Latina.* Buenos Aires
Sandoval, Alonso de
1956   *De instauranda aethiopum salute: El mundo de la esclavitud negra en América.* Bogotá
Santa Gertrudis, Juan de
1956   *Maravillas de la naturaleza,* I. Bogotá
Sapper, Karl
1924   "Die Zahl und die Volksdichte der indianischen Bevölkerung in Amerika," *Proceedings of the Twenty-first International Congress of Americanists* (The Hague)
Sayers, Raymond
1956   *The Negro in Brazilian Literature.* New York
Scelle, George
1906   *La traité négrière aux Indes de Castille.* Paris
Scheuss de Studer, Elena F.
1958   *La trata de negros en el Río de la Plata durante el siglo XVIII.* Buenos Aires
Schmidel, U.
1938   *Derrotero y viaje a España y las Indias.* Transl. and comments by E. Wernicke. Santa Fe (Argentina)
Shapiro, Harry
1953   *Race Mixture.* Paris

Sicroff, Albert A.
1960   Les controverses des statuts de "pureté de sang" en Espagne
                    du XVᵉ au XVIIᵉ siècle. Paris
Skinner-Klee, J. (ed.)
1954   Legislación indigenista de Guatemala. Mexico (Instituto In-
                    digenista Interamericano)
Smith, T. Lynn
1966   "The Racial Composition of the Population of Colombia,"
                    Journal of Inter-American Studies, VIII
Solórzano y Pereira, Juan de
1647   Política Indiana. Madrid
Sommers, Joseph
1964   "The Indian-Oriented Novel in Latin America: New Spirit,
                    New Forms, New Scope," Journal of Inter-American Studies,
                    VI
Spinden, H. J.
1928   "The Population of Ancient America," Geographic Review,
                    XVIII
Stabb, Martin S.
1959   "Indigenism and Racism in Mexican Thought, 1857–1911,"
                    Journal of Inter-American Studies, I
1957   "Martí and the Racists," Hispania, XL (Baltimore, Md.)
Stavenhagen, Rodolfo
1963   "Clases, colonialismo y acculturación," América Latina, VI
                    (Rio de Janeiro)
Stein, Stanley
1961   "Freyre's Brazil Revisited," The Hispanic American Historical
                    Review, XLI
1964   "Historiografía latinoamericana: balance y perspectivas," His-
                    toria Mexicana, XIV
1957   Vassouras: A Brazilian Coffee County. Cambridge, Mass.
Stewart, Watt
1951   Chinese Bondage in Peru. Durham, N.C.
Stonequist, Everett V.
1937   The Marginal Man: A Study in Personality and Culture Con-
                    flict. New York
Straten Ponthoz, Auguste van der
1854   Le budget du Brésil . . . , III. Brussels
Strickom, Arnold
1965   "Hacienda and Plantation in Yucatán: An Historical-Eco-
                    logical Continuum in Yucatán," América Indígena, XXV
                    (Mexico)
Tannenbaum, Frank
1947   Slave and Citizen: The Negro in the Americas. New York
Teixeira Soares
1961   O Marquês de Pombal: A lição do passado e a lição do
                    pressente. Rio de Janeiro
Tigner, J. L.
1963   "The Ryukyuans in Bolivia," The Hispanic American His-
                    torical Review, XLIII
1961   "Shindō Remmei: Japanese Nationalism in Brazil," The His-
                    panic American Historical Review, XLI

171

Tingsten, Herbert
1950   *Revolutionernas arvtagare*. Stockholm, Sweden
Tjarks, Germán
1958   "Juan Larrea y la defensa de los naturales," *Publicaciones del Museo de la Casa de Gobierno*, series I:7 (Buenos Aires)
Torre Revello, José
1927   "Esclavas blancas en las Indias Occidentales," *Boletín del Instituto de Investigaciones Históricas*, VI (Buenos Aires)
1932   "Origen y aplicación del Código Negrero en la América española, 1788–1794." *Boletín del Instituto de Investigaciones Históricas*, XV (Buenos Aires)
Torres Quintero, Gregorio
1921   *México hacia el fin del virreinato español*. Paris and Mexico
Vallenilla Lanz, Laureano
1961   *Cesarismo democrático: Estudios sobre las bases sociológicas de la constitución efectiva de Venezuela*, 4th ed. Caracas
Varallanos, José
1962   *El cholo y el Perú*. Buenos Aires
Vasconcelos, José
1942   *Vasconcelos*. Ed. by G. Fernández MacGregor. Mexico
Vázquez, Mario C.
1961   *Hacienda, peonaje y servidumbre en los Andes Peruanos*. Lima
1964   *The Castas: Unilinear Kin Groups in Vicos, Peru*. Cornell University 1964. Multigr.
Vázquez-Machicado, Humberto
1956   "Orígenes del mestizaje en Santa Cruz de la Sierra," *Universidad de San Carlos*, XXXVI (Guatemala)
Vega, Inca Garcilaso de la
1959   *Comentarios Reales de los Incas*. Buenos Aires and Lima
Véliz, Claudio
1961   *Historia de la marina mercante de Chile*. Santiago
Vellard, Jean
1956   "Causas biológicas de la desaparición de los indios americanos," *Boletín del Instituto Riva Agüero* (Lima)
Verlinden, Charles
1964?   "Esclavage médiéval en Europe et esclavage colonial en Amérique," *Cahiers de l'Institut des Hautes Études de l'Amérique Latine*, VI (Paris)
1955   *L'esclavage dans l'Europe médiévale: I. Péninsule Ibérique. France*. Bruges
Vial Correa, Gonzalo
1947   *El africano en el Reino de Chile: Ensayo histórico-jurídico*. Santiago
Viana Filho, Luis
1940   "O trabalho do engenho e a reacção do índio," *Congresso do Mundo Portugues, Publicações*, X (Lisbon)
Vicens Vives, Jaime (ed.)
1957–1958   *Historia social y económica de España y América*, II–IV: I. Barcelona
Villalobos, Sergio
1962   "El comercio extranjero a fines de la dominación española," *Journal of Inter-American Studies*, IV

Villa-Señor y Sánchez, J. A.
1748   Theatro Americano: Descripción general de los reynos y
            provincias de la Nueva España, I–II. Mexico
Wagley, Charles (ed.)
1952   Race and Class in Brazil. Paris.
─────── and Marvin Harris
1958   Minorities in the New World: Six Case Studies. New York
Waibel, Leo
1955   Die europäische Kolonisation Südbrasiliens. Bonn
Warren, Donald
1965   "The Negro and Religion in Brazil," Race, VI (London)
Willems, Emílio
1946   A aculturação dos alemães no Brasil: Estudo antropológico dos
            immigrantes alemães e seus descendentes no Brasil. São
            Paulo
Williams, Eric
1944   Capitalism and Slavery. Chapel Hill, N.C.
Wolf, Eric R.
1962   Sons of the Shaking Earth. Chicago
1957   "The Mexican Bajío in the Eighteenth Century," Synoptic
            Studies of Mexican Culture, New Orleans
─────── and Sidney Mintz
1957   "Haciendas and Plantations in Middle America and the An-
            tilles," Social and Economic Studies, VI (Kingston, Jamaica)
Wolff, Inge
1964   "Negersklaverei und Negerhandel in Hochperu, 1545–1640,"
            Jahrbuch für Geschichte von Staat, Wirtschaft und Ge-
            sellschaft Lateinamerikas, I (Cologne)
Zavala, Silvio
1945   Contribución a la historia de las instituciones coloniales en
            Guatemala. Mexico (Jornadas, 36)
1940   De encomiendas y propriedad territorial en algunas regiones
            de la América Latina española. Mexico
1948   Estudios indianos. Mexico
1944   "Los orígenes del peonaje en México," Trimestre económico,
            X (Mexico)
─────── and María Castelo (ed.)
1946   Fuentes para la historia del trabajo en Nueva España, VII.
            Mexico
Zelinsky, Wilbur
1949   "The Historical Geography of the Negro Population of Latin
            America," The Journal of Negro History, XXXIV
Zulueta, Eduardo
1916   "Movimiento antiesclavista en Antioquia," Boletín de His-
            toria y Antigüedades, X (Bogotá)
Zum Felde, Alberto
1959   Índice crítico de la literatura hispanoamericana, I–II. Mexico

Index

174